SINGER

SEWING REFERENCE LIBRARY®

Sewing with Knits

Cy DeCosse Incorporated
Minnetonka, Minnesota

SINGER

SEWING REFERENCE LIBRARY®

Sewing with Knits

Contents

Copyright © 1992
Cy DeCosse Incorporated
5900 Green Oak Drive
Minnetonka, Minnesota 55343
1-800-328-3895
All rights reserved
Printed in U.S.A.

SEWING WITH KNITS
Created by: The Editors of Cy DeCosse
Incorporated, in cooperation with
the Sewing Education Department,
Singer Sewing Company. Singer is a
trademark of The Singer Company and
is used under license.

Library of Congress
Cataloging-in-Publication Data

Sewing with knits.

p. cm. — (Singer sewing reference
library)
Includes index.
ISBN 0-86573-268-X
ISBN 0-86573-269-8 (pbk.)
1. Machine sewing. 2. Knit goods.
I. Cy DeCosse Incorporated. II. Series.
TT715.S49 1992
646.4'04— dc20   91-34345

Distributed by: Contemporary Books, Inc.
  Chicago, Illinois

CY DECOSSE INCORPORATED
Chairman: Cy DeCosse
President: James B. Maus
Executive Vice President: William B. Jones

Also available from the publisher:
*Sewing Essentials, Sewing for the Home,
Clothing Care & Repair, Sewing for Style,
Sewing Specialty Fabrics, Sewing
Activewear, The Perfect Fit, Timesaving
Sewing, More Sewing for the Home,
Tailoring, Sewing for Children, Sewing
with an Overlock, 101 Sewing Secrets,
Sewing Pants That Fit, Quilting by
Machine, Decorative Machine Stitching,
Creative Sewing Ideas, Sewing Lingerie,
Sewing Projects for the Home*

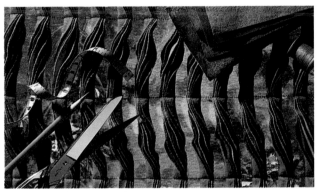

Executive Editor: Zoe A. Graul
Technical Director: Rita C. Opseth
Project Manager: Linda Halls
Senior Art Director: Delores Swanson
Writer: Rita C. Opseth
Contributing Writer: Nancy Restuccia
Editors: Janice Cauley, Bernice Maehren
Sample Coordinator: Carol Olson
Technical Photo Director: Bridget Haugh
Styling Director: Bobette Destiche
Fabric Editor: Joanne Wawra
Research Assistant: Lori Ritter
Sewing Staff: Phyllis Galbraith, Bridget
  Haugh, Sara Holmen, Marilyn Krell,
  Linda Neubauer, Carol Olson, Carol
  Pilot, Wendy Sotebeer, Nancy Sundeen,
  Barb Vik

*Director of Development, Planning
  & Production:* Jim Bindas
Photo Studio Managers: Rebecca Boyle,
  Cathleen Shannon, Rena Tassone
Lead Photographers: Rex Irmen, Mette
  Nielsen
Photographers: John Lauenstein, Mark
  Macemon, Mike Parker, Cathleen
  Shannon, Phil Aarrestad, Kim Bailey,
  Doug Deutscher, Charles Nields
Production Manager: Amelia Merz
Electronic Publishing Analyst:
  Kevin D. Frakes
Production Staff: Joe Fahey, Peter Gloege,
  Melissa Grabanski, Jim Huntley, Mark
  Jacobson, Daniel Meyers, Linda
  Schloegel, Greg Wallace, Nik Wogstad

Consultants: Cindy Curtis, Ann Fatigati,
  Wendy Fedie, Pamela Hastings, Barbara
  Kelly, Judy Laube, Connie Long, Julie
  Muschamp
Contributors: Burda Patterns, Inc.;
  Butterick Patterns; Coats & Clark Inc.;
  Dyno Merchandise Corp.; Everitt
  Knitting Mills; Laube's Stretch & Sew,
  Inc.; The McCall Pattern Company;
  Minnetonka Mills, Inc.; Nancy's
  Notions, Ltd®; Simplicity Pattern Co.
  Inc.; Swiss-Metrosene, Inc.; Treadle
  Yard Goods; Vogue Patterns
Color Separations: La Cromolito
Printing: Ringier America, Inc. (0492)

Introduction

When you sew with knits, you can sew more clothes in less time. Knits are ravel-free and require little pressing, making them easy to sew and care for. Whether you are new to knit sewing or discovered it long ago, this book will give you tips for handling the fabrics and ideas for updated garment details.

Consider all the possibilities for sewing with knits, from the wide variety of fabric types to the different pattern designs. In the Getting Started section of this book, you will learn about single-knit and double-knit construction and discover a variety of knit fabrics, including the basic jerseys and interlocks as well as the elegant panne stretch velvets and the sporty spandex blends. Learn how to select a pattern that is right for your fabric, checking the amount of stretch in the fabric against the stretch gauge of the pattern. Then assemble and prepare the fabric, pattern, and notions, and get ready to cut.

Turn to the Basic Sewing Techniques section for step-by-step guidance in sewing seams, hems, and garment edges. Whether you sew on the conventional sewing machine or on an overlock machine, you will learn how to sew seams that stretch with the fabric to prevent the stitches from breaking. And when it is necessary to preserve the shape of the garment, learn how to stabilize the seams. Hems, which are subjected to stress during wear, can also stretch with the fabric; sew hems that are inconspicuous, or topstitch them to add detailing to the garment edge. Learn how to apply the popular ribbing trim to your garments; ribbed edges can be sewn using either the flat or

in-the-round method of construction. Or for another look, try bound edges instead of ribbing.

In the Easy Wardrobes section, gain confidence in sewing with knits by making T-shirts, tank tops, skirts, pants, and cardigan jackets. Included in this section are the fastest and easiest methods for assembling great-looking clothes. Whether you are a beginning sewer or have sewn most of your life, you will be surprised by all the garments you can make in such a short time.

In the section, Easy Design Variations, you will see new design details that can change the look of basic patterns. Learn new ways to finish necklines, from soft and drapable cowls to modified V necks. Try some new pocket styles, including ribbed-edge patch pockets and window pockets; there's even an easy-to-sew welt pocket. Elasticized waistbands, which can be both functional and attractive, are also included in this section. Create a wearable work of art by layering and slashing knit fabrics for a unique garment. Or embellish a garment with twisted knit trim for a creative accent.

The Specialty Knits section introduces you to napped fabrics, sweater knits, and two-way stretch knits. Whether you want a sumptuous, soft velour pullover, a crewneck sweater, or a body-hugging cotton/spandex skirt, you will be given helpful advice for handling the special fabrics. This section also takes you through the steps for sewing and fitting swimsuits, leotards, and tights.

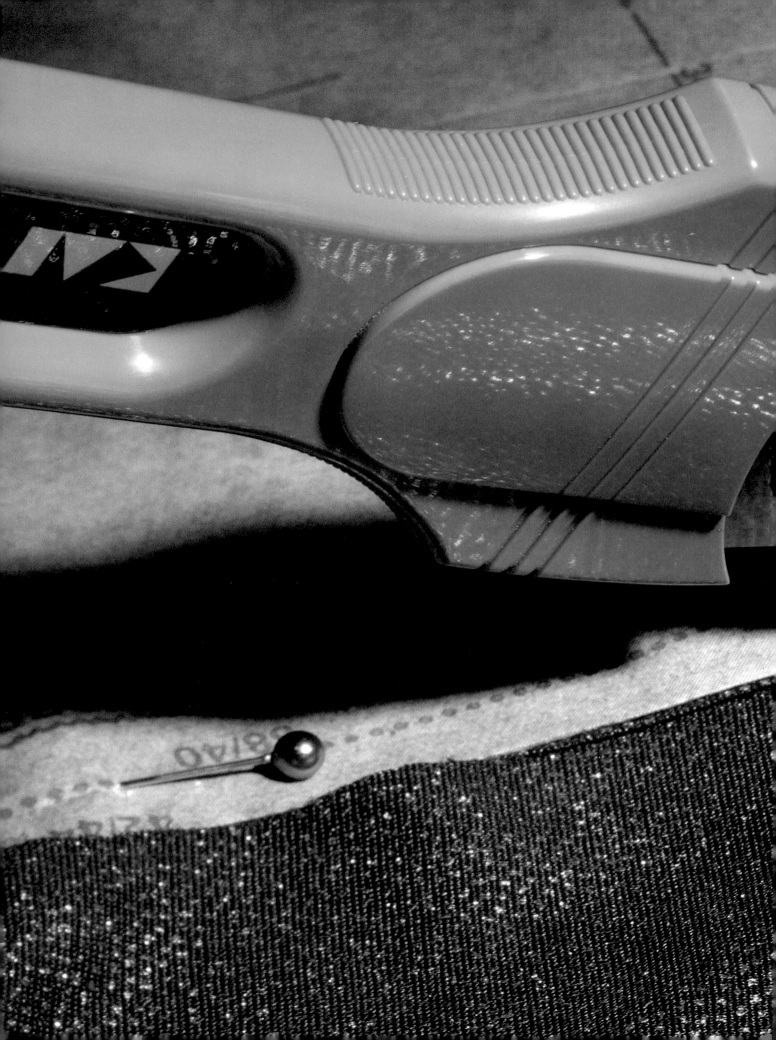

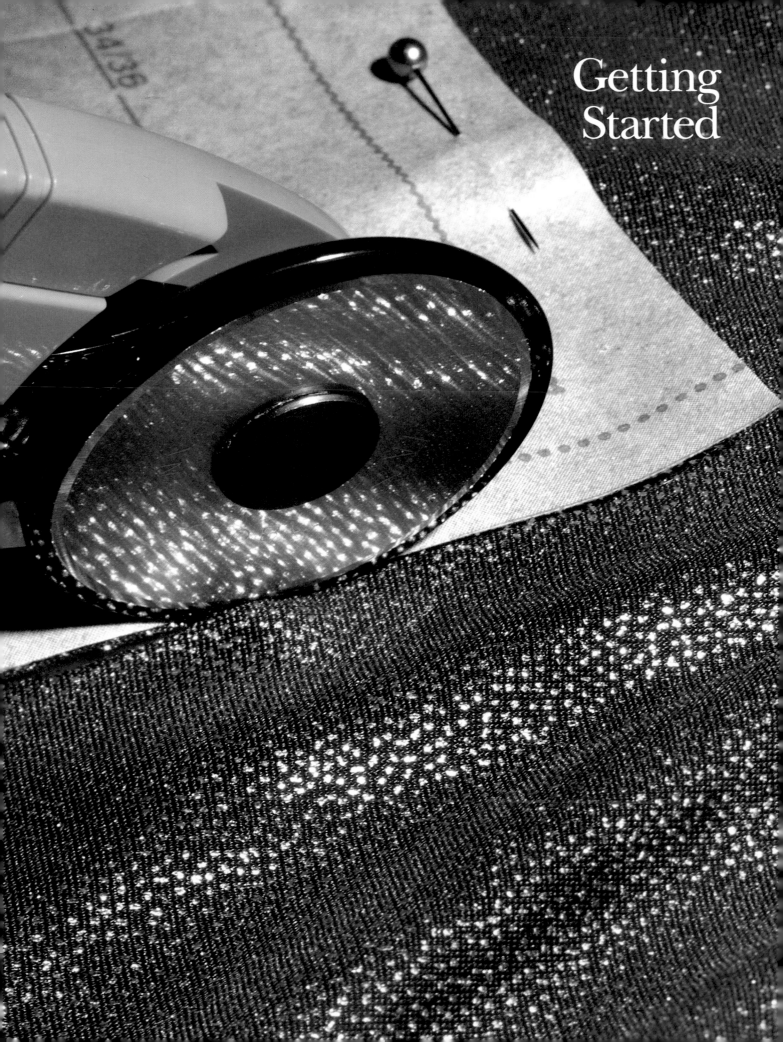

Getting
Started

Selecting & Sewing Knits

Knits are easy to sew and comfortable to wear. They are available in many colors, prints, and fibers. Knits can be used to sew a wide variety of garments, including casual pants and tops for daywear, dresses and suits for the office, tights and swimsuits for activewear, and gowns for evening wear.

It is easier to fit garments made from knits than those made from woven fabrics, because knits stretch and designs for knit garments tend to have less complicated lines. Construction is easier and seam finishes are often unnecessary, because knits generally do not ravel. Clothing made from knit fabrics requires less care than most garments sewn from woven fabrics.

Feel the fabric to determine the drapability, wrinkle-resistance, stretch, and recovery. Check for any runs, snags, or other flaws. Look for permanent creases or fading along the fold of the fabric. Note the percentage of shrinkage listed on the end of the bolt; allow extra fabric, if necessary.

Before purchasing fabric, check the grainline. For best results when sewing garments, the lengthwise ribs and crosswise courses (right) should be perpendicular to each other; knit fabrics cannot be straightened.

Fiber Content

Knit fabrics are available in a wide variety of fibers. As you select fabrics, notice the fiber content listed on the end of the bolt.

Fabrics made from natural fibers are comfortable, because they are absorbent and breathe well. All-cotton knits are soft, durable, and readily available in a wide variety of colors, weights, and textures. Wool knits hold their shape well. Knits made from silk, linen, and rayon may require special care during construction and cleaning.

Fabrics made from synthetic fibers are generally easy to care for. They can usually be washed and dried by machine, take brilliant dyes, and resist fading and wrinkling. They are not absorbent, so, while they dry quickly, they do not breathe well and may develop static electricity. Widely available synthetics include nylon, polyester, and acrylic.

Blends combine fiber characteristics. When natural and synthetic fibers are blended, the result is a fabric more resistant to shrinkage and wrinkling than a fabric made from natural fibers only. It is also less absorbent, which can be an advantage. The less moisture a fabric holds, the more quickly the garment dries when wet. But, the higher the percentage of synthetic fiber, the less the fabric allows perspiration to evaporate.

Spandex is an elastic synthetic fiber that is covered with yarns made of other fibers. Spandex gives a knit fabric added stretch and the ability to retain its shape.

Knit Construction

Knit fabric is made from interlocking looped stitches. The lengthwise rows of stitches are called *ribs;* the crosswise rows are called *courses.* These ribs and courses correspond to the lengthwise and crosswise grains of woven fabrics.

Single-knit construction is used for several types of fabrics. One set of needles is used to manufacture the fabric. Single-knit fabrics are characterized by flat vertical ribs on the right side and dominant horizontal courses on the wrong side. The fabrics stretch crosswise but have little lengthwise stretch. When the crosswise edge of a single-knit fabric is stretched, it curls to the right side.

Double-knit construction is also used for several types of fabrics. Two sets of needles are used, making fabric that is double in thickness. Fabrics made using this process have a finely ribbed surface that is the same on both sides. They are usually stable or have only moderate stretch. Although fabrics made with double-knit construction range from very soft to very firm, the term "double knit" frequently refers to a firm knit fabric (opposite).

Jersey, also known as "single knit," is one of the fabric types made by single-knit construction (opposite). It has flat vertical ribs on the right side of the fabric and dominant horizontal courses on the wrong side. Jersey has little lengthwise stretch and is often used for shirts, dresses, and lingerie.

Double knits are usually firm, plain knits, although some may be striped or textured. Medium to heavy in weight, they are stable or have only moderate stretch. Because they have firm body, they are especially suitable for jackets, suits, and pants.

Interlocks have a very fine rib on both sides and are lightweight to mediumweight, with a soft, supple hand. They usually have moderate crosswise stretch. Runs may occur in one direction. Interlocks are used to make T-shirts, sportswear, and sleepwear.

Sweatshirt fleece has flat vertical ribs on the right side and a soft, brushed surface on the wrong side. It is usually stable, with little stretch in either direction. Sweatshirt fleece is adaptable to a wide variety of simple designs and is most often used for sweatshirts, sweatpants, and other sporty garments.

Sweater knits range from smooth
and lightweight to lofty and bulky.
They are available by the yard and
as sweater bodies (page 107). They
have a nap and may run. Sweater
knits are most suitable for sweaters
and loose-fitting dresses and skirts.

Ribbings have prominent vertical
ribs on both sides. They have a
significant amount of stretch,
which makes them particularly
suitable for finishing garments at
necklines, waistlines, leg openings,
armholes, and the lower edges of
sleeves. Ribbings are sometimes
used for close-fitting garments.

Two-way stretch knits include spandex, an elastic synthetic fiber. The knits stretch both lengthwise and crosswise and have excellent recovery. Spandex is often blended with polyester, cotton, or nylon. Frequently used for form-fitting garments such as swimwear, leotards, and leggings, two-way stretch fabrics may be used for a variety of other garments.

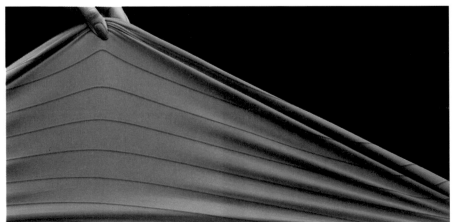

Knit terries, including stretch terry and French terry, have small loops on the right side and smooth vertical ribs on the wrong side. French terry is heavier and more stable than stretch terry. When stitched right sides together, terries tend to shift, because of their nap.

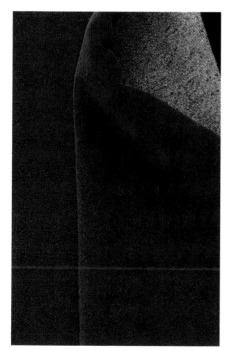

Velours, available in various weights, have a soft, brushed nap on the right side and smooth vertical ribs on the wrong side. Like knit terries, velours may shift when stitched right sides together.

Stretch velvets have a brushed nap on the right side and smooth vertical ribs on the wrong side. The napped surface of stretch velvet has a shinier appearance than velour. Stretch panne, shown, is a type of stretch velvet with a crushed appearance. Placed right sides together, stretch velvets shift easily during stitching.

Mesh knits are knitted with evenly spaced holes. They do not ravel or run, but can be snagged. Generally, they are used as an inset or overlay to add surface texture to a garment, or as ventilation in activewear.

Novelty knits range in appearance from sheer and lacy to heavy and coarse. The degree of stretch varies, depending on the design and type of yarn used.

Selecting a Pattern

Choose a pattern according to the weight, texture, and stretch characteristics of the fabric. If a knit is soft and lightweight, like jersey, it is suitable for a pattern that features gathers or draping. If it is a bulky or textured fabric, a pattern with few seams and details works best to minimize bulk.

Patterns designed for knits take into consideration how much the knit will stretch, so the amount of ease allowed is usually less than that in a pattern designed for wovens. Patterns labeled "for stretch knits only" require knit fabrics that stretch a specific amount. Although most knit fabrics stretch to some degree, the amount of stretch can vary considerably, depending on the fiber content and the type of knit. Test the fabric against the gauge printed on the back of the envelope to determine if it has sufficient stretch, as shown below.

Patterns for garments such as swimsuits, leotards, or leggings are labeled "for two-way stretch knits only,"

and require fabrics blended with spandex. Test both the lengthwise and the crosswise stretch to determine whether the fabric is suitable for the pattern.

Some patterns designed for woven fabrics may also be used for knits. Because these patterns do not allow for the stretch of a knit, select a stable or moderate-stretch knit, avoiding fabrics that might stretch out of shape.

When sewing with knit fabrics, measure your body accurately to ensure a proper fit, referring to the guidelines for taking measurements, given in the pattern catalog. Compare your body measurements to those on the pattern envelope to select the correct size. For knit tops, sweaters, dresses, and one-piece swimsuits, select the pattern size based on your bust measurement. For skirts, shorts, pants, and leggings, select the size based on your hip measurement.

How to Use a Stretch Knit Gauge on a Pattern

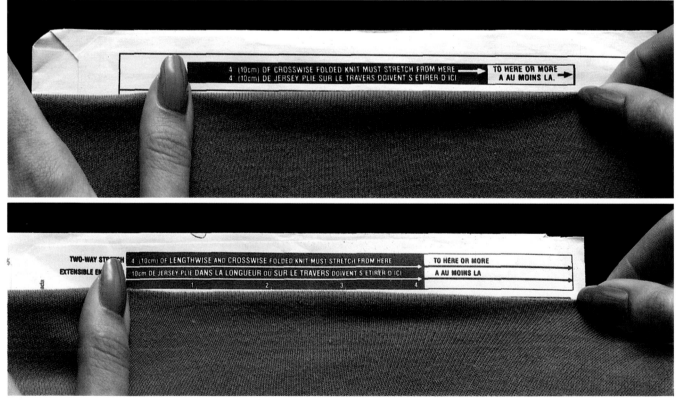

Fold over the crosswise edge of knit fabric 3" to 4" (7.5 to 10 cm). Stretch fabric along fold against gauge printed on pattern envelope. If the pattern is appropriate for the fabric, the fabric will stretch to the right-hand side of the gauge (top). If fabric must be stretched beyond reasonable limits, distorting the ribs (bottom), the pattern is not appropriate for the fabric.

Preparing the Fabric

For best results, pretreat knit fabrics before you cut out the pattern, using the same care method you intend to use for the finished garment. Refer to the label on the end of the fabric bolt for the manufacturer's recommended instructions.

If the fabric is washable, prewash and dry it, using soap or detergent to remove excess dye and surface finishes that may cause stitching problems. Before washing a knit that could ravel, such as a sweater knit, zigzag or overlock the fabric along the raw edges. To prevent wrinkling, place a few dry towels in the dryer with the fabric and remove the fabric promptly after it is dry. When machine drying a synthetic knit fabric, use a low setting on the dryer.

Some knits, particularly cotton, may continue to shrink slightly with each successive washing. This *residual shrinkage* can usually be prevented by washing the fabric and drying it thoroughly at a medium setting two or three times before cutting out the pattern.

Generally, ribbing should not be washed if it is to be used as a trim. When prewashed, ribbing becomes softer, making it more difficult to cut small pieces accurately. However, if you are using a dark-colored ribbing as a trim on a light-colored fabric, soak the ribbing in a vinegar and water solution to remove any excess dye, and allow it to air dry.

If you intend to dry-clean the garment, pretreat the fabric by thoroughly steam pressing it from the wrong side, then leaving it flat until completely dry. Or, have the fabric steamed by a professional dry cleaner. Pretreat sweater knits that require dry cleaning by blocking the fabric as shown at left.

If a knit fabric requires pressing, press it lightly in the direction of the lengthwise ribs, taking care not to stretch the knit out of shape.

After pretreating the fabric, check it for any lines caused from creasing or fading or from finishes applied by the manufacturer. Creases can sometimes be removed by steam pressing. Lines caused from fading or finishes, however, are permanent and should be avoided or positioned inconspicuously when laying out the pattern.

How to Block Sweater Knits

Pat sweater-knit yardage or sweater body into shape on a flat surface. Steam fabric, using a steam iron or hand steamer held above surface of knit. Allow fabric to cool and dry completely before handling.

Preparing the Pattern

Adjust the pattern, if necessary, before laying out and cutting the pattern pieces. For a multisize pattern, compare your body measurements to the chart on the pattern envelope to determine which size to use in each area of the pattern. Length adjustments may be made on the pattern pieces, along the adjustment lines on the pattern.

Patterns designed for knits often have ¼" (6 mm) seam allowances. Check the pattern to be sure you know what size seam allowances are included. Before cutting, add wider seam allowances in areas where you anticipate fitting adjustments may be needed.

Tips for Preparing the Pattern

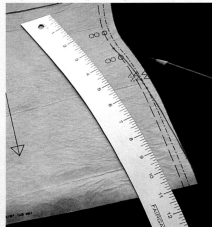

Mark points on the pattern that correspond to the pattern size you are using in each area. Redraw cutting lines by connecting points and smoothing curves.

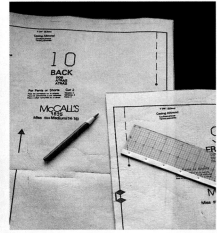

Make seam allowances wider in areas where fitting adjustments may be needed.

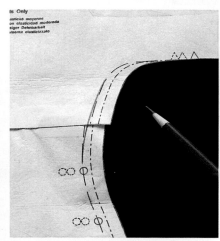

Cut pattern on adjustment lines. Keeping grainline straight, lap pattern to shorten it. Or spread pattern to lengthen it, taping tissue paper in place under pattern, as shown at top of page. Redraw seamlines and cutting lines.

Interfacings & Elastics

After selecting the fabric and the pattern, select any necessary interfacing or elastics for the garment. Keep in mind the type of fabric you are sewing and the garment style when you make the selections.

Selecting Interfacing

Interfacings are used minimally on knit fabrics, because garment designs for knits tend to be less structured. Interfacings are used where stretch is not desired and in faced areas where support is needed to maintain the shape of the garment, such as at necklines, plackets, buttonholes, and pockets. Choose lightweight interfacings, either knit or nonwoven, that do not change the character of the knit fabric.

Fusible nonwoven interfacings (a) may stretch in all directions and are appropriate for knits, provided the interfacings are lightweight, soft, and supple.

Fusible knit interfacings (b) are frequently used for knits. They stretch only in the crosswise direction.

Nonfusible knitted interfacings (c) are also suitable for knits; these interfacings are soft and sheer, yet they are stable and provide body. They may also be used instead of the garment fabric for pocket facings.

Preshrink interfacings by hand washing them gently and allowing them to air dry; or steam press them just before they are applied to the fabric. When interfacing is used on faced garment edges, apply it to the facing, rather than the garment, to prevent show-through. Fusible interfacing may be applied to the fabric before you cut out the pattern piece to save time and to prevent shifting.

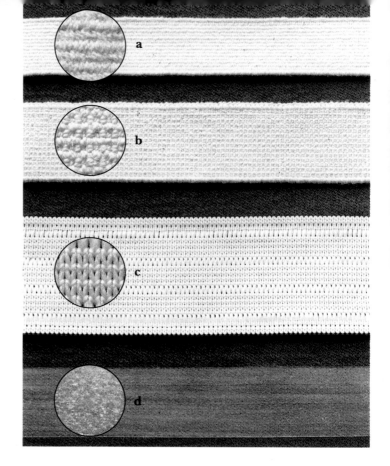

Selecting Elastic

There are various types of elastics, each with different stretch and recovery characteristics. They are suitable for different applications, depending on the type and fiber content.

Braided elastics (a) have prominent lengthwise ridges and become narrower when stretched. Because they are firm, they are suitable for casing application methods. Cotton braided swimwear elastic is chlorine-resistant and salt-resistant. Because of its excellent stretch and recovery, it may be used for stitched-on or topstitched applications in swimwear as well as other garments.

Woven elastics (b) retain their width when stretched and have a square-gridded surface texture. Cotton woven elastic is fairly stable and is suitable for casing applications. Polyester woven sports elastic is suitable for stitched-on or topstitched applications.

Knitted elastics (c) are relatively soft, making them suitable for stitched-on or topstitched applications only. When used in casings, they tend to twist or roll. They retain their width when stretched and are distinguished by the "V" pattern of the knit. Some knitted elastics have a drawstring through the center and are used for waistbands in active sportswear.

Transparent elastic (d) stretches three to four times its length and has complete recovery. It is best suited for stitched-on or topstitched applications, especially for lingerie and swimwear. Transparent elastic also works well to stabilize seams in knit garments.

Needles & Thread

When sewing knits, you can often prevent snagged fabrics, skipped stitches, puckered seams, and thread breakage by using the correct needle and thread.

Selecting Needles

Choose the smallest needle size appropriate for the fabric you are sewing. For lightweight knits, use a size 70/9. For mediumweight knits, use a size 80/11. For heavy and bulky knits, use a size 80/11 or a 90/14. If skipped stitches occur, try a new needle or change to a different size.

Three basic types of machine needles are available: ballpoints, universals, and sharps. Selecting the correct needle type for the fabric you are sewing is as important as selecting the correct size.

Ballpoint needles have rounded tips. They penetrate knit fabrics by separating, rather than piercing, the yarns, preventing snags.

Universal needles are modified ballpoint needles. The tip of a universal needle is more tapered than that of a ballpoint needle. Universal needles can be used on many fabrics, knit or woven.

Sharps can be used on knits with open or loose textures, but are most commonly used for sewing woven fabrics. Sharps are not suitable for firm, tightly knitted fabrics or knits made from heavy polyester or nylon fibers. It is difficult for sharps to pierce these knits, and the needle often breaks the fibers, leaving holes.

An overlock machine, or serger, may require special needles; refer to the manual for your machine. If your overlock machine uses standard needles, select either ballpoints, universals, or sharps, as above.

It is helpful to have double and triple needles when sewing knits on the conventional sewing machine. For multiple stitching on seams and topstitched hems, these needles allow you to sew two or three perfectly even rows of stitches in one step.

Double needles have two needles on one shank. They are numbered according to both needle size and width of spacing. A size 2.0/80 double needle, for instance, has two size 80/11 needles, spaced 2 mm apart. Universal and ballpoint double needles are available in a variety of sizes. Generally, the heavier the fabric, the larger the needle, and the wider the space between the needles. For knits, use double needles set at least 2 mm apart.

Triple needles have three needles on one shank. They are numbered by the needle size and the width between the two outer needles. For knits, the 3.0/80 size works well.

Selecting Thread

Synthetic-fiber thread is well suited for sewing knits because of its strength and inherent stretch. The most frequently used threads are polyester or cotton-wrapped polyester. All-purpose thread, either polyester or cotton-wrapped polyester, is used on mediumweight to heavyweight fabrics. Extra-fine thread should be used for sewing lightweight knits. For use on an overlock machine, polyester and cotton-wrapped polyester thread is available on cones. Woolly nylon thread, available only on cones, may be used on an overlock machine for sewing soft, comfortable seams in mediumweight to heavyweight knits.

Wind synthetic-fiber thread onto the bobbin slowly to prevent stretching it. If wound at high speed, it may stretch enough to cause puckered seams.

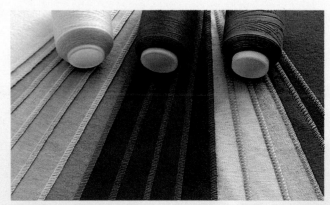

Woolly nylon thread is available in a limited number of colors, but it is not necessary to have an exact color match for each project. Ivory, rose, and gray blend with most fabric colors.

Laying Out & Cutting the Pattern

When laying out and cutting pattern pieces on knits, always use a "with nap" pattern layout. Knits have a directional quality that shows up as a difference in color shading in the completed garment.

Stretch both crosswise edges of a knit before laying out the pattern to see if the knit runs. Runs will occur more readily along one edge than the other. Position the run-prone edge at the garment hemline when laying out pattern pieces. The hem is subjected to less stress during construction, so the fabric will be less likely to run.

If the fabric has a flaw, such as a permanent crease or line, position pattern pieces to avoid the flaw, whenever possible. If you cannot avoid it, position it in an inconspicuous area of the garment. If the fabric is knit as a tube, cut the fabric, following a lengthwise rib, along any permanent crease or line before laying out the pattern.

Do not allow the fabric to hang off the work surface when laying out the pattern pieces. The weight of the fabric can distort the portion on the work surface, pulling it off-grain.

Fabric can be cut as a double layer with one or two folds, or as a single layer. Cut a double layer of fabric with one foldline when laying out larger pattern pieces. However, for efficient use of the fabric, two foldlines may allow you to place the front and back pieces of a garment across from each other. When cutting bulky, textured, slippery, or patterned fabrics, it is easier and more accurate to lay out the pattern on a single layer of fabric, cutting one half at a time. Secure pattern pieces with weights, or with pins pushed straight down through the pattern and fabric seam allowances into a cardboard or padded surface.

Mark knits, using a water-soluble marking pen, pins, or chalk. If you are using a marking pen, mark the pieces within the seam allowance, unless you are sure the ink can be completely removed. On knits that do not run, notches may be marked with 1/8" (3 mm) clips into 5/8" (1.5 cm) seam allowances.

If both sides of the fabric look similar, mark the wrong side of each garment piece with transparent tape before removing the pattern pieces.

How to Cut Knits Using the Double-layer Method

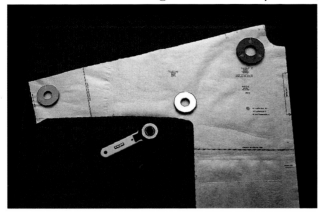

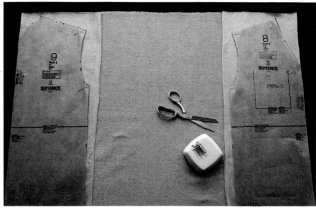

Single fold. Fold fabric in half along lengthwise rib, smoothing out fabric; selvages may not match. Position pattern pieces; secure with weights or pins. Cut fabric, using rotary cutter or bent-handle shears.

Double fold. Fold fabric along lengthwise rib, so double layer of fabric is wide enough to accommodate pattern piece. Fold remaining fabric along rib. Position pattern pieces; secure with weights or pins. Cut the fabric, using rotary cutter or bent-handle shears.

How to Cut Knits Using the Single-layer Method

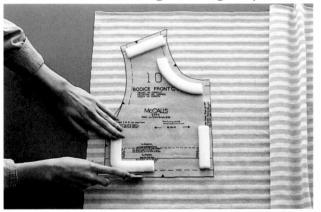

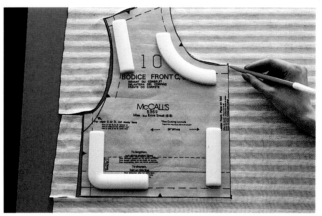

1) Spread the fabric on work surface, right side up. Position pattern piece; secure with weights or pins. Cut out first half of garment section, using a rotary cutter or bent-handle shears.

2) Mark center line of pattern piece at top and bottom, within seam allowances. Remove pattern piece. Fold cut garment section along center line, matching stripes or pattern.

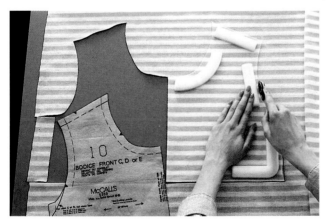

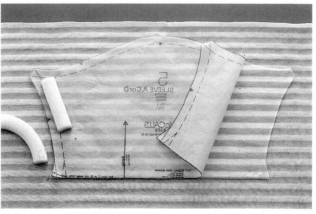

3) Lay pattern piece over garment section if fabric is loosely woven; check shape, adjusting as necessary. Remove pattern piece. Cut second half of garment section, following raw edges of top fabric layer.

4) Lay out any pattern piece that needs to be cut twice, on single layer of fabric; cut. Remove pattern piece. Turn garment section over, and lay pattern piece on top, shaping fabric; use as a guide for cutting next piece.

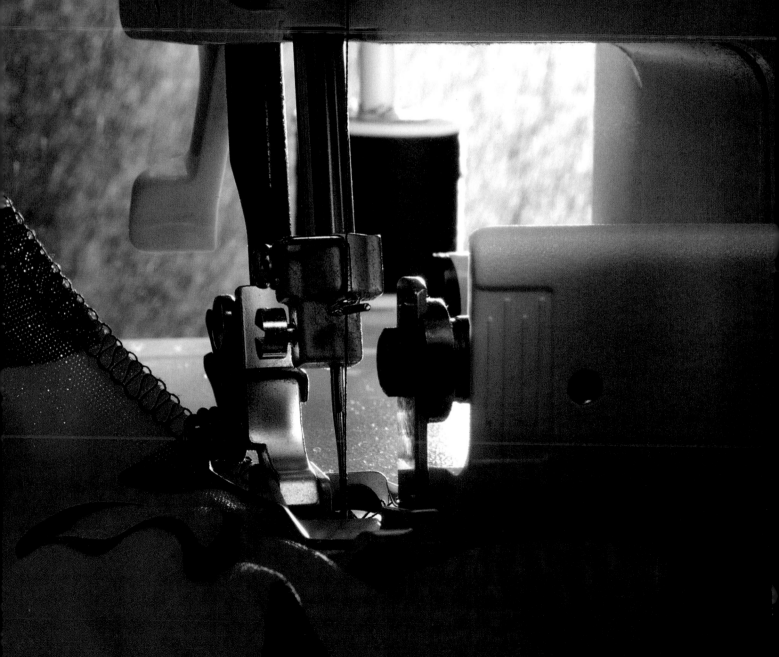

Basic Sewing
Techniques

Seams & Seam Finishes

When knit fabrics are stretched, the seams also have to stretch to prevent the stitches from breaking. The seams may be stitched using a conventional sewing machine or an overlock machine. Knit fabrics normally do not fray, making seam finishes unnecessary.

Conventional Seams

Straight-stitch seams, sewn using a stretch-as-you-sew technique, are suitable for stable or moderate-stretch knits. After the seam is stitched, the knit fabric relaxes to its original position. In the finished garment, the pressed-open seams have the necessary give to prevent stitches from breaking when stressed.

Zigzag seams have built-in stretch, due to the nature of the zigzag stitch, and are suitable for all knits. The seams are sewn using a narrow, short zigzag stitch, then pressed open.

Double-stitched seams are narrow, ¼" (6 mm) seams with two rows of straight stitching or zigzag stitching. If straight stitches are used, the fabric is stretched as you sew to build stretch into the seam. The seam allowances are pressed to one side.

Double-needle seams are stitched with a double needle. Suitable for all knits, they get their stretch from the zigzag formed by the bobbin thread as it alternates between needle threads on the underside.

Stretch-stitch seams are strong and elastic. Stretch stitches are particularly well suited for stitching seams that will receive heavy stress during wear and for sewing stretchy fabrics. Test a stretch stitch before using it in the garment; some reverse-action stretch stitches may be so dense that they make the seams stiff.

Overlock Seams

3-thread and 4/3-thread overlock seams are narrow stretch seams sewn on a serger. For maximum stretch, use a 3-thread overlock stitch, and, for moderate stretch, a 4/3-thread overlock stitch. Use a wider stitch for mediumweight and heavyweight knits to provide greater strength and to secure yarn floats; use a narrower stitch on lightweight knits to prevent puckering or tunneling. The overlock stitch also works well as an edge finish for lightweight knit fabrics that have a tendency to curl. The stitching helps the seam allowances lie flat.

Flatlock seams are flat, stretchy seams, sewn using the flatlock stitch on a serger. When the fabric is stitched wrong sides together, the loops of the flatlock stitch show on the right side of the garment for a decorative, sporty look. When stitched right sides together, the ladder side of the flatlock stitch shows on the right side; the ladders hide in the texture of sweater knits for a smooth, nonbulky seam.

Stabilized Seams

In some areas of a garment, it is necessary to limit the amount of stretch in the seams to preserve the shape of the garment or to make the seams more durable. Shoulder, crotch, and waistline seams of knit garments are often stabilized.

Bias-binding stabilized seams use tricot bias binding to prevent shoulder seams and waistline seams in lightweight to mediumweight fabrics from stretching out of shape. Bias binding is also recommended for crotch seams, to add strength to the seams.

Elastic stabilized seams use transparent elastic to prevent shoulder seams or waistline seams in mediumweight to heavyweight fabrics from stretching out of shape.

Topstitched stabilized seams may be used for shoulder and waistline seams in any fabric weight, to prevent the seams from stretching and to keep the seam allowances flat. On pressed-open seams, topstitch next to the seamline on both sides. On seams that are pressed to one side, topstitch through the seam allowance layers next to the seamline.

Tips for Sewing Knit Seams

Prevent the raw edges of lightweight fabrics from curling as you sew by applying spray starch to the seam allowances and pressing them before stitching the seams.

Prevent distorted or rippled seams by reducing the pressure on the presser foot. This can be done by pressing down on the back of the presser foot with your thumb, lifting the front of the foot, as shown opposite. Or adjust the pressure bar on the sewing machine.

Prevent fabrics that require matching, such as striped fabrics, from shifting by basting the seam allowances together with water-soluble glue stick, basting glue, or basting tape.

Prevent knit fabrics from bunching at the beginning of a seam by holding the thread tails under and behind the presser foot, then lowering the foot. Do not backstitch at the beginning of the seam; tie the thread tails after the seam is stitched.

Reduce bulk on seams that meet by pressing them open or in opposite directions.

Seams, shown top to bottom, are: straight-stitch conventional seam, bias-binding stabilized seam, and 3-thread overlock seam.

Five Ways to Sew Seams in Knits Using a Conventional Machine

Straight-stitch seam. Stitch 5⁄8" (1.5 cm) seam, using straight stitch on conventional machine set at 9 to 12 stitches per inch (2.5 cm); gently stretch fabric as you sew. Fabric feeds through machine in stretched position; do not pull fabric through. Press seam open.

Zigzag seam. Stitch 5⁄8" (1.5 cm) seam, using short, narrow zigzag stitches; do not stretch fabric as you sew. Push down lightly with thumb on back of presser foot, lifting front of foot, if necessary, so fabric feeds smoothly. Press seam open.

Double-stitched seam. Stitch first along seamline, as for straight-stitch or zigzag seams, left; then stitch again 1⁄8" (3 mm) from first row of stitches, within seam allowance. Trim excess seam allowance close to second row of stitches.

(Continued on next page)

Five Ways to Sew Seams in Knits Using a Conventional Machine (continued)

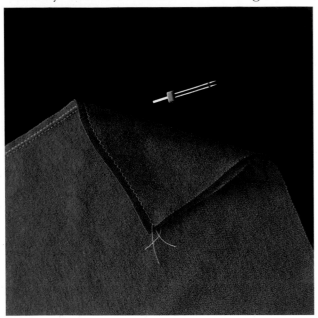

Double-needle seam. Stitch seam, using double needle, with left needle along seamline and right needle within seam allowances; do not stretch fabric. Test stitching on scrap; adjust needle thread tension, if necessary. If tension is too tight, a ridge occurs between stitching lines; if too loose, bobbin thread does not zigzag, reducing stretch. Press seam to one side.

Stretch-stitch seam. Stitch ¼" (6 mm) seam, using stretch stitch, with left edge of stitch along seamline; do not stretch fabric. Use overedge foot, if available. (Stretch stitches vary, depending on make and model of sewing machine, as shown above.)

Two Ways to Sew Seams in Knits Using an Overlock Machine

3-thread or 4/3-thread overlock seam. Adjust serger for 3-thread or 4/3-thread overlock stitch. Stitch seam, right sides together, trimming excess seam allowance with knives.

Flatlock seam. Adjust serger for flatlock stitch. Stitch seam, trimming excess seam allowance with knives. Pull crosswise on seam, pulling stitches flat. Stitch seam *wrong* sides together for decorative seam on sportswear **(a)**; stitch seam *right* sides together for flat seam on sweater knits **(b).**

Three Ways to Sew Stabilized Seams in Knits

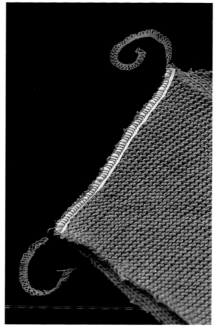

Bias-binding stabilized seam. Cut a strip of tricot bias binding the length of seam; place over seam. Stitch through relaxed strip, using conventional or overlock method. Trim excess binding close to stitching, if desired.

Elastic stabilized seam. Cut a strip of transparent elastic the length of seam; place over seam. Stitch through relaxed strip, using conventional or overlock method. Trim excess elastic close to stitching, if desired.

Topstitched stabilized seam. Stitch seam; press open **(a)**, or press to one side **(b)**. From right side, topstitch next to seamline through garment and seam allowances.

How to Press Seams in Knits

1) Press seam flat, right sides together, in direction it was stitched, to embed stitches. Ease fabric back into shape if seamline was distorted during stitching.

2) Open seam, or fold to one side. Hold steam iron above fabric; steam momentarily. Flatten seam, using clapper or hands. Steam from right side to flatten seam; use iron guard or press cloth to prevent shine, if necessary.

Hems

Inconspicuous hems on knits may be hand-stitched, using the catchstitch. Or they may be machine-stitched on either a conventional or overlock sewing machine, using the blindstitch. Machine blindstitches become embedded in knit fabrics, especially bulky or textured knits, for an almost invisible hem.

On many knit garments, hems do not need to be inconspicuous. Topstitching with a single, double, or triple needle adds interest and decorative detailing in addition to being durable, functional, and quick. Topstitching is suitable on many different styles of garments, from sportswear to career wear. The stitch length frequently used for topstitching is about 8 to 10 stitches per inch (2.5 cm).

Tips for Hemming Knit Garments

Press the hem into place before stitching by lowering and lifting the iron from the fabric. Allow the pressed section to dry before handling to prevent stretching the fabric.

Place tape on the bed of the sewing machine to serve as a guide for the folded edge of the fabric.

Prevent distorted or rippled hems by reducing the pressure on the presser foot. This can be done by pressing down on the back of the presser foot with your thumb, lifting the front of the foot, as shown on page 29. Or adjust the pressure bar on the sewing machine.

Stretch the fabric slightly when using single-needle topstitching in areas that will be subjected to stress. It is not necessary to stretch the fabric when topstitching with a double or triple needle.

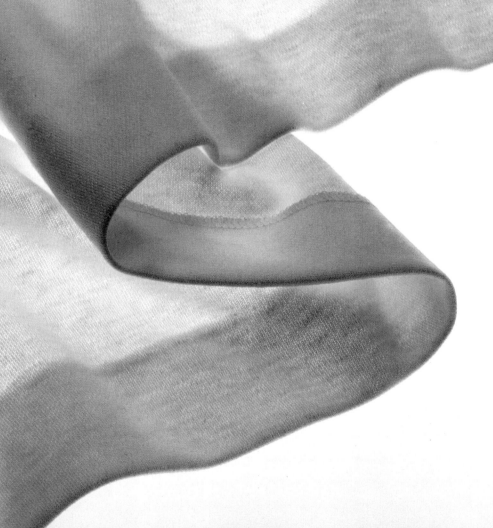

Catchstitched hem. Overlock raw edge, if desired; press hem in place. Fold back hem edge. Working from left to right, catch fabric alternately at hem edge and garment, using small needle and taking small backstitches. Space stitches ⅜" (1 cm) apart. Stretch fabric slightly before knotting thread ends.

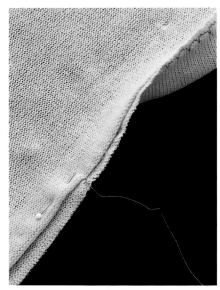

Blindstitched hem. Overlock raw edge, if desired; press hem in place. Fold hem allowance back to right side of garment, with hem edge extending ⅜" (1 cm) beyond fold. Using blindstitch setting on conventional sewing machine, stitch on extended hem edge. Adjust stitch width and stitch length to barely catch fold with swing of needle, about every ⅜" (1 cm).

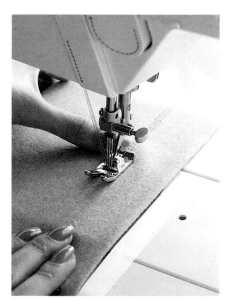

Topstitched hem. Overlock raw edge, if desired; press hem in place. Stitch through both layers from right side; double or triple needle is recommended for built-in stretch, but single needle may be used on stable knits. If raw edge is not overlocked, trim close to stitching from wrong side.

Ribbed Edges

The most common use for ribbing is to finish the edges of knit sportswear garments. Ribbing, which has great crosswise stretch and recovery, enables garment openings to stretch easily when you are getting dressed and return to a neat, comfortable fit during wear. Ribbing is available as yardage and as prefinished ribbed bands.

Ribbing yardage ranges in width from 28" to 60" (71 to 152.5 cm), or 14" to 30" (35.5 to 76 cm) tubular, and is available in several weights. To use ribbing yardage, cut a crosswise strip of the fabric, fold it in half lengthwise, and apply it so the fold becomes the finished edge.

Prefinished ribbed bands have one finished edge and are applied as a single layer. They are available in various widths and lengths. They also come in different weights and styles.

Ribbing can be used as an edge finish for several styles of necklines, including turtleneck, mock turtleneck, crewneck, and scoop-neck. It is also used on sleeves, lower edges of T-shirts and sweatshirts, and waistlines of pants and skirts. The cut width and cut length of the ribbing varies, depending on where it will be used and the style you want.

If you use ribbing yardage, the cut width of the ribbing is equal to twice the desired finished width plus ½" (1.3 cm) for seam allowances. If you use prefinished ribbed bands, the cut width is equal to the desired finished width plus one ¼" (6 mm) seam allowance.

Many patterns designed for knits indicate what length to cut the ribbing, or they provide a pattern piece to be used as a guide for the ribbing pieces. The cut length for ribbing can also be determined by measuring the garment opening at the seamline, as shown below.

For straight, close-fitting edges, the cut length can be determined by pin-fitting the ribbing on the body. On any straight edges that do not require a close fit, such as the lower edge of a skirt, cut the ribbing just slightly shorter than the garment edge.

To sew ribbed edges, you may use either the flat or the in-the-round method of construction. Flat construction is the fastest method; however, the seams may be noticeable at the edges of the ribbing. For a better-quality finish, the in-the-round method is usually preferred. With this method, the ribbing seams are enclosed for a neater appearance.

If matching ribbing is not available, self-fabric, cut on the crosswise grain, can be substituted for ribbing yardage. Use a knit fabric that stretches at least 50 percent crosswise; for example, 10" (25.5 cm) of knit must stretch to at least 15" (38 cm).

How to Determine the Cut Length

Measure seamline of garment opening by standing tape measure on edge. For necklines, cut ribbing as on page 36. For other garment openings, ribbing is usually cut two-thirds of the measurement plus ½" (1.3 cm). If self-fabric is substituted for ribbing, cut it three-fourths of measurement plus ½" (1.3 cm).

Pin-fit ribbing or self-fabric around body for straight, close-fitting edges, such as at hiplines, wrists, and ankles. Fold ribbing crosswise for double thickness, and pin ribbing so it lies flat, without gaping; do not distort the ribs. Add ½" (1.3 cm) for seam allowances.

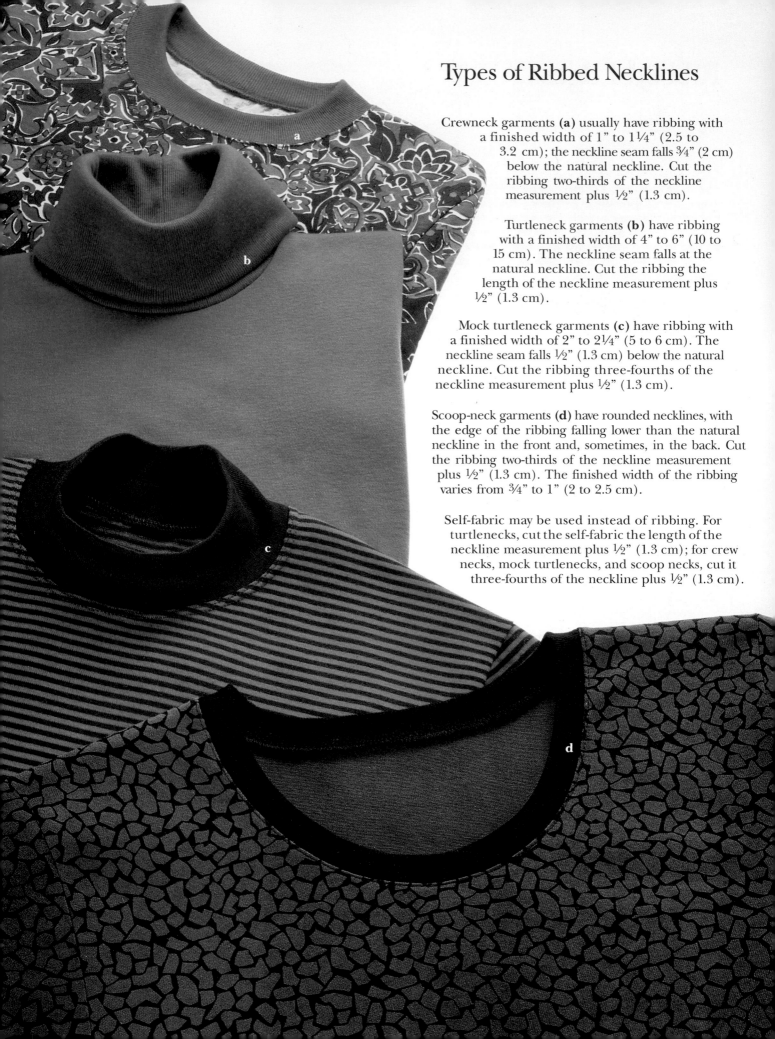

Types of Ribbed Necklines

Crewneck garments (a) usually have ribbing with a finished width of 1" to 1¼" (2.5 to 3.2 cm); the neckline seam falls ¾" (2 cm) below the natural neckline. Cut the ribbing two-thirds of the neckline measurement plus ½" (1.3 cm).

Turtleneck garments (b) have ribbing with a finished width of 4" to 6" (10 to 15 cm). The neckline seam falls at the natural neckline. Cut the ribbing the length of the neckline measurement plus ½" (1.3 cm).

Mock turtleneck garments (c) have ribbing with a finished width of 2" to 2¼" (5 to 6 cm). The neckline seam falls ½" (1.3 cm) below the natural neckline. Cut the ribbing three-fourths of the neckline measurement plus ½" (1.3 cm).

Scoop-neck garments (d) have rounded necklines, with the edge of the ribbing falling lower than the natural neckline in the front and, sometimes, in the back. Cut the ribbing two-thirds of the neckline measurement plus ½" (1.3 cm). The finished width of the ribbing varies from ¾" to 1" (2 to 2.5 cm).

Self-fabric may be used instead of ribbing. For turtlenecks, cut the self-fabric the length of the neckline measurement plus ½" (1.3 cm); for crew necks, mock turtlenecks, and scoop necks, cut it three-fourths of the neckline plus ½" (1.3 cm).

How to Sew Ribbed Edges (flat method)

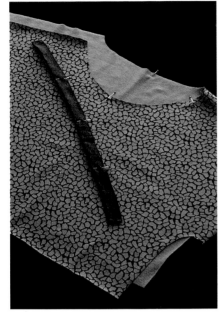

1) Cut garment pieces, allowing ¼" (6 mm) seam allowances at garment openings. Leave one seam unstitched. If using ribbing yardage, fold ribbing in half lengthwise, wrong sides together. Divide ribbing and garment opening into fourths; pin-mark.

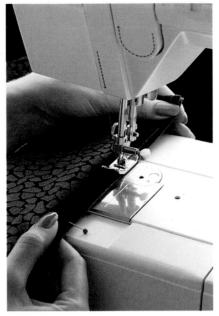

2) Pin ribbing to right side of garment, matching pin marks. With ribbing on top, stitch ¼" (6 mm) seam, using narrow zigzag or overlock stitch; stretch ribbing to fit garment opening as you sew. Lightly press seam toward garment.

3) Stitch remaining garment seam, matching ribbing seam and ends carefully. If desired, topstitch close to seamline as in step 3, below.

How to Sew Ribbed Edges (in-the-round method)

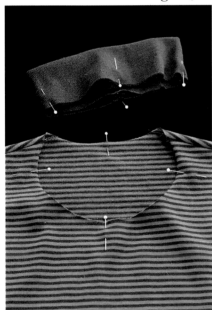

1) Join ends of ribbing in ¼" (6 mm) seam. If using ribbing yardage, fold ribbing in half lengthwise, wrong sides together. Divide ribbing and garment opening into fourths; pin-mark.

2) Pin ribbing to right side of garment, matching pin marks. With ribbing on top, stitch ¼" (6 mm) seam, using narrow zigzag or overlock stitch; stretch ribbing to fit garment opening as you sew. Lightly press seam toward garment.

3) Topstitch close to seamline, if desired, stitching through garment and seam allowances, using single or double needle. If single needle is used, stretch fabric slightly as you sew.

Variations for Ribbed Edges

Ribbed edges can be varied in a number of ways to add detailing and interest to garments. Although these techniques give a variety of looks, they all use basic in-the-round construction.

Double ribbing **(a),** used at the neckline and the lower edges of sleeves, gives the look of two shirts in one. For this effect, two pieces of ribbing are cut to different widths and applied in one step to the garment opening.

A lapped neckline **(b)** features ribbing overlapped at the center. For women's and girls' garments, the right

end of the ribbing laps over the left; for men's and boys' garments, the left end laps over the right.

A contrasting self-fabric insert **(c)** can accent the center front of a ribbed neckline or waistline. For added detailing, decorative topstitching can be added to the insert.

Striped ribbing **(d)** is made by stitching two or three pieces of ribbing together for a multicolor trim. This ribbed trim is especially suitable for mock turtlenecks and the lower edges of sleeves and T-shirts.

How to Apply Double Ribbing

1) Cut two pieces of ribbing to length determined for garment opening (page 35). Cut one ribbing piece 3" (7.5 cm) wide for a finished width of 1¼" (3.2 cm); cut the other piece 2½" (6.5 cm) wide for a finished width of 1" (2.5 cm).

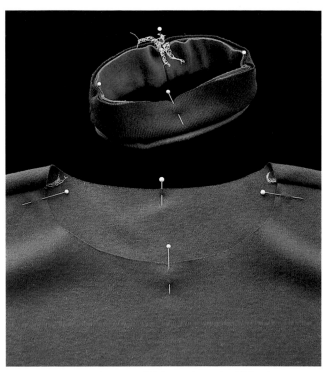

2) Stitch ends of each ribbing piece in ¼" (6 mm) seam. Fold each piece in half lengthwise, wrong sides together. Pin narrow ribbing over wide ribbing, with raw edges even and seams matching. Divide ribbing and garment opening into fourths; pin-mark.

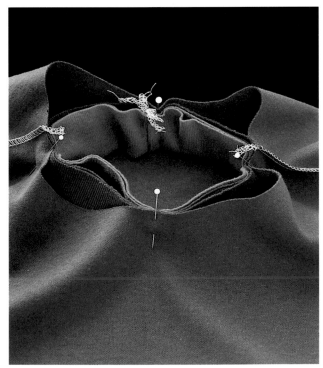

3) Pin double ribbing to garment, matching pin marks, with right sides together, raw edges even, and ribbing seams at center back of neckline or underarm seam of sleeve. Narrow ribbing will be next to garment.

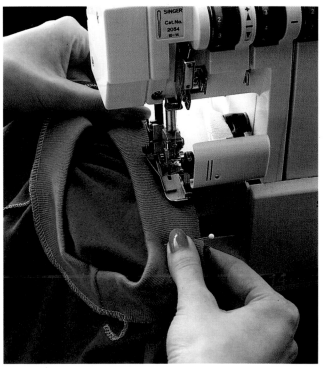

4) Stitch neckline in ¼" (6 mm) seam, with ribbing on top, using overlock stitch or narrow zigzag; stretch ribbing to fit garment opening as you sew. Lightly press seam toward garment. Edgestitch, using single, double, or triple needle, if desired.

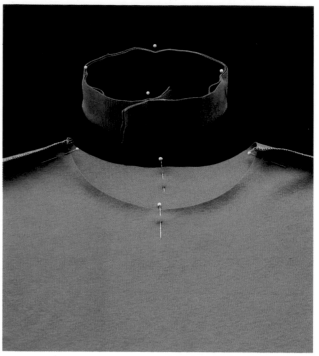

1) Cut ribbing to desired cut width by 2" (5 cm) longer than length determined for garment opening (page 35). Fold in half lengthwise. Measure in 1" (2.5 cm) from each end; pin-mark.

2) Lap ends, matching pin marks; this is center front. Divide ribbing into fourths; repeat for garment opening, with one pin at center front.

3) Pin ribbing to right side of garment, matching pin marks and center fronts, with raw edges even. (Woman's garment is shown.)

4) Curve ends of ribbing into seam allowance, so folded ends overlap and taper to raw edges.

5) Release center pin so garment neckline relaxes to natural curve. Repin at center front. Trim excess fabric. Stitch as on page 39, step 4.

How to Apply Ribbing with a Self-fabric Insert

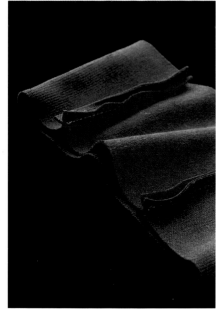

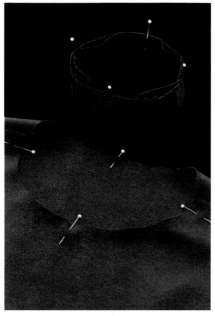

1) Cut ribbing to desired cut width by 3" (7.5 cm) shorter than length determined for garment opening (page 35). Cut insert fabric to same width as ribbing by 3½" (9 cm) long. Stitch insert to ribbing at short ends in ¼" (6 mm) seams, forming a circle.

2) Fold ribbing/insert in half lengthwise, wrong sides together. Divide ribbing/insert into fourths; pin-mark, with one pin marking center front at middle of insert. Divide garment opening into fourths; pin-mark, with one pin at center front.

3) Pin ribbing/insert to garment, with right sides together and raw edges even; match center fronts and pin marks. Stitch as on page 39, step 4. Topstitch through all layers of insert, if desired.

How to Apply Striped Ribbing

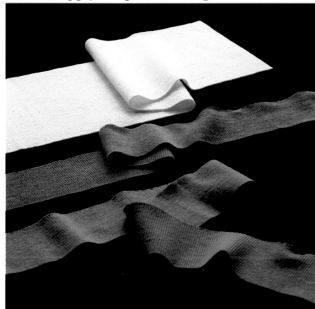

1) Cut strips to length determined for garment opening (page 35). The cut width of each strip is desired finished width of strip plus ½" (1.3 cm) for seam allowances; also add finished width of pieced strip to color at outer edge to allow for back of ribbing. Join long ends of strips, right sides together, in ¼" (6 mm) seams; lightly press to one side.

2) Join short ends in ¼" (6 mm) seam; lightly press. Fold in half lengthwise, wrong sides together. Divide ribbing and garment opening into fourths; pin-mark. Pin ribbing to garment, matching pin marks, with right sides together, raw edges even, and ribbing seam at center back of neckline or underarm seam of sleeve. Stitch as on page 39, step 4.

Bound Edges

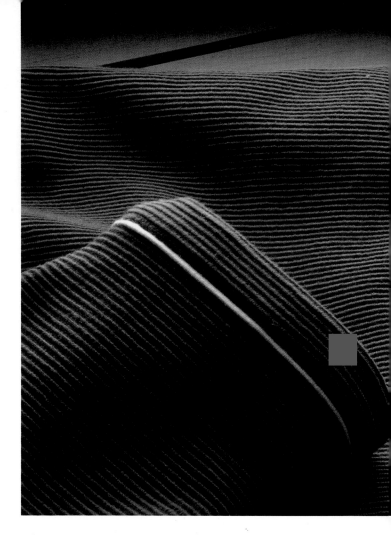

Bound edges are a popular finish for knit garments, especially T-shirts and tank tops. Using matching or contrasting binding, you can quickly and easily add a decorative touch to a garment. With one additional step, flat piping may be added to the binding for a special effect.

Binding can serve as an alternative to facings and hems. For lightweight and light-colored fabrics, it eliminates any possibility of show-through, which can occur with a facing or hem. When heavier fabric is used, binding is less bulky than facings and hems.

Because binding has a limited amount of stretch, it is used only on garment openings that can be pulled easily over the head, or for garments with zippered or buttoned closures. The finished binding should be ½" (1.3 cm) wide, so it will lie flat.

The basic method for bound edges, shown here, is frequently used, because it is the easiest to sew and results in a binding with minimal bulk. To eliminate bulk, the edge of the binding is not folded under on the wrong side of the garment. If both the right and wrong sides of the garment edge will show, as in a cardigan, you may prefer French binding (pages 63 to 65), which has enclosed edges on both sides.

When using this basic method for binding a circular edge, such as the neckline of a pullover or the lower edge of a sleeve, a combination of flat and in-the-round construction is used. One garment seam is left unstitched until after the binding strip is attached. Then the final seam is stitched, and the binding is wrapped around the garment edge to the inside, enclosing the seam. If the bound edge will end at a hemline or facing, the ends of the binding are finished as shown on page 45.

For the binding, cut strips of self-fabric or ribbing on the crosswise grain. Or if striped fabric is used, the strips may be cut on the bias for diagonally striped binding. For ½" (1.3 cm) finished binding, the cut width of the binding strips is 1⅞" (4.7 cm). The combined length of the strips is equal to the distance around the edge to be bound plus about 3" (7.5 cm) to allow for finishing the ends and easing the binding around outer curves; the strips may be pieced together as necessary.

For binding with flat piping, cut fabric strips for the piping on the crosswise grain, with a cut width of 1¼" (3.2 cm). The combined length of the strips is equal to the distance around the edge to be bound plus about 3" (7.5 cm) to allow for finishing the ends and easing the binding around outer curves; the strips may be pieced together as necessary.

How to Apply Binding on Circular Edges

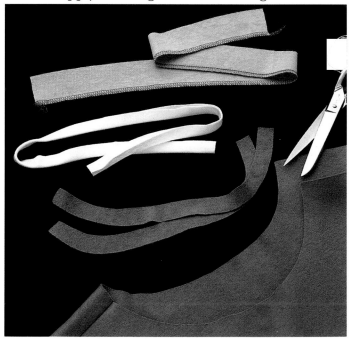

1) **Trim** seam allowances from garment opening. Construct garment, leaving one seam unstitched at edge to be bound. Staystitch neck edge, if desired, as on page 51. Overlock one long edge of binding strip, if desired.

2) **Press** piping strip in half lengthwise, wrong sides together, if binding with flat piping is desired. Pin piping to right side of garment, with raw edges even; machine-baste ½" (1.3 cm) from raw edge.

3) **Align** unfinished edge of the binding to edge of the garment, right sides together. Stitch seam, with seam allowance equal to finished width of binding. Ease binding at outside curves, or stretch binding slightly at inside curves.

(Continued on next page)

4) Trim piping, if added, close to stitching. Trim excess binding at ends even with garment fabric. Lightly press binding away from garment, with seam allowances toward binding.

5) Stitch remaining garment seam, stitching through binding. If using double-stitched seam **(a)**, end second row of stitching at binding; clip seam open in binding area, and press. If using overedge or overlock seam **(b)**, press the seam, changing direction of seam in binding area.

6) Fold binding over raw edges to wrong side of garment; secure with glue stick or liquid basting glue or by pinning in the ditch of the seam.

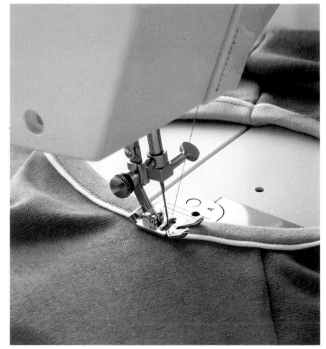

7) Stitch along edge of binding from right side, using single, double, or triple needle, depending on desired effect. If edge of binding is not overlocked, trim binding close to stitching.

How to Apply Binding with Finished Ends

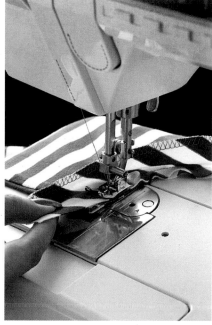

1) Trim seam allowances from garment opening. Overlock one long edge of binding strip, if desired. Attach binding as on page 43, steps 2 and 3, leaving ends of binding and piping extending ½" (1.3 cm) beyond finished edge of garment.

2) Trim piping, if added, close to stitching. Lightly press binding away from garment, with seam allowances toward binding. At ends, fold binding, right sides together, positioning fold even with raw edges. Stitch ends; trim.

3) Fold binding as in step 6, opposite; tuck under raw edge of binding at each end. Finish as in step 7, opposite.

How to Apply Binding with Inside Corners

1) Staystitch for 1" (2.5 cm) on each side of inside corner, using short stitch length, with distance from garment edge to staystitching equal to finished width of binding. Clip to stitching at corner.

2) Make and apply binding as on pages 42 and 43, steps 1 to 3. While stitching, straighten garment edge at corner and keep edges even. It is easier to stitch inside corners if garment fabric is on top.

3) Follow steps 4 to 7, opposite; in step 7, straighten corner. Fold garment at corner, right sides together, matching bound edges. Miter corner by stitching through binding in line with fold.

Easy
Wardrobes

Easy Wardrobes

You can sew a year-round wardrobe of knit garments quickly and easily, even if sewing with knits is new to you. If you already have experience sewing with knits, you can make clothes faster than ever, using the easy techniques on the following pages. Start by sewing a variety of T-shirts and tank tops. Then go on to make the skirts and pants they team up with. Mixed and matched, even a few garments can expand your wardrobe.

Adapt these basic instructions to create different styles. By varying the neckline, garment length, or

sleeve length, for example, you can change the look of a T-shirt. The easy, pull-on skirts can vary from close-fitting minis to full, gathered, calf-length styles. And pull-on pants can range from shorts or culottes to ankle-length pants. This wardrobe even includes a cardigan jacket with French binding. For best results, select knit fabrics that have good body and recovery. Knits with good recovery are always the easiest to sew. Interlock, sweatshirt fleece, and stretch terry are frequently used for casual wear. For dressier garments, use knit fabrics such as wool jersey or panne velvet.

Easy Tank Tops

Tank tops are quick and easy to make and are versatile additions to any wardrobe. Sew a number of them in different colors and fabrics to accent many of your outfits. Wear them alone, layered over other tanks or T-shirts, or under big shirts or jackets for a variety of looks.

A tank top can be constructed quickly, using a simple turned-and-stitched edge finish for the curved armhole and neck edges. Staystitching the neckline and armholes is an important step in this construction technique. During construction, the staystitching serves as a guide for pressing and stitching. During wear, it helps prevent the garment from stretching out. The result is a better-looking tank top, because the neckline and armhole openings tend to hug the body rather than gape.

Cut out the garment pieces with ½" (1.3 cm) seam allowances at the neckline and armholes. Mark the center front and center back at the neck edge. Before sewing the tank top, you may want to baste the front and back sections together and check the fit.

How to Sew a Tank Top

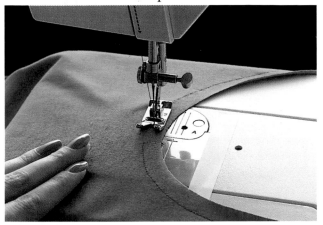

1) Staystitch a scant ½" (1.3 cm) from neck edge on garment front, beginning at shoulder and ending at center front, using short straight stitches, about 12 to 15 stitches per inch (2.5 cm). Do not stretch fabric as you sew. Repeat for opposite side, overlapping a few stitches at center. Repeat for garment back.

2) Staystitch a scant ½" (1.3 cm) from armhole edge on garment front, beginning at shoulder. Do not stretch fabric as you sew. Repeat for opposite side, then for garment back.

3) Stitch garment together at shoulders. If desired, overlock raw edges at neckline and armholes, trimming ⅛" (3 mm).

4) Press seam allowances on armholes and neckline to wrong side, using staystitching as a guide; stitching should not show on right side. Use steam and a clapper to press folds flat. Stitch side seams.

5) Topstitch ⅛" and ¼" (3 and 6 mm) from folded edges, using single needle. Or topstitch ¼" (6 mm) from folded edges, using double or triple needle. Trim raw edges, if desired. Stitch hem (pages 32 and 33).

Cropped T-shirt of printed interlock has hemmed lower edge and sleeves. The self-fabric neckline trim is applied using the method for ribbed edges (pages 35 to 37).

T-shirts & Other Pullovers

T-shirts and other pullovers are staples in wardrobes today. All sewn in the same basic way, patterns are available in a variety of looks, from classic crewneck styles to oversized cropped tops to career dresses. Construct a classic T-shirt with a ribbed neck edge, and make several, varying the look by changing the ribbing (pages 35 to 37). Add shoulder pads (page 55), if desired, using hook and loop tape. The same pair of shoulder pads can be used with many T-shirts.

For more variety, add ribbing instead of hems to the lower edges and sleeves of T-shirts, following the alternate method on page 55. For close-fitting ribbed edges, pin-fit the ribbing on your body or cut it to two-thirds the length of the garment edge. For a looser fit, cut the ribbing slightly smaller than the garment edge. Topstitching next to the ribbed seams can also add detailing to T-shirts.

Ribbing can be applied to T-shirts using either the flat or in-the-round method of construction. The in-the-round method, shown on pages 54 and 55, is recommended for neat, enclosed ribbing seams. If you are adding ribbing to the sleeves or the lower edge, however, you may want to use the flat method (page 37) for quick construction. Although the seams in the ribbing are not enclosed when flat construction is used, they are less noticeable at these edges than at the neckline.

Cut out the garment pieces, allowing ¼" (6 mm) seam allowances; allow wider seam allowances at the side seams if fitting adjustments may be needed. Allow 1" to 2" (2.5 to 5 cm) hem allowances at the lower edge of the garment and at the lower edges of short sleeves. Allow ⅝" to 1" (1.5 to 2.5 cm) hem allowances for long sleeves. Cut the ribbing as on pages 35 and 36.

Short T-shirt, made from printed interlock, has ribbing trim. The ribbing on the sleeves and the lower edge is stretched slightly as it is applied.

Hip-length pullover, made from interlock, features wide ribbing at the lower edge. For a snug fit, the ribbing is cut to two-thirds the measurement of the garment opening.

Pullover dress, made from wool jersey, has hemmed edges. The detachable shoulder pads are applied using hook and loop tape.

How to Sew a T-shirt

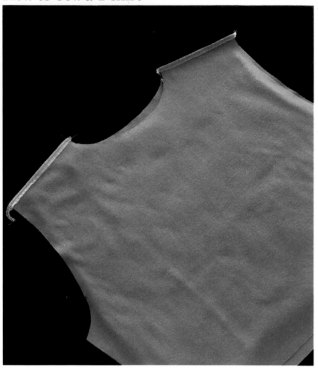

1) **Stitch** stabilized shoulder seams (page 31); if using tricot bias binding or transparent elastic, place it on garment front. From right side, press seam allowances toward garment back.

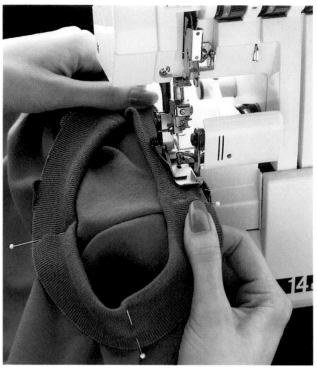

2) **Attach** ribbing to neckline of garment, using the in-the-round method on overlock or conventional machine (page 37).

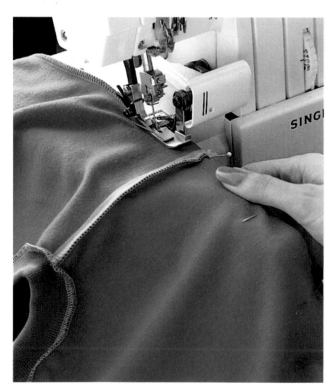

3) **Stitch** sleeves into armholes, right sides together. Press seam allowances toward sleeves. Or press seam allowances toward body of garment; topstitch, using single, double, or triple needle.

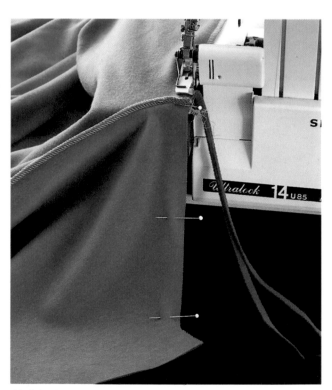

4) **Stitch** one side and sleeve seam, right sides together, stitching from lower edge of garment to lower edge of sleeve, matching underarm seam. Repeat for other side and sleeve seam. Press seam allowances toward garment back.

5) Hem sleeves and lower edge of garment, using topstitched or blindstitched method (page 33).

Alternate method. Follow steps 1 to 4, opposite. Apply ribbing to sleeves and lower edge of T-shirt, using in-the-round method (page 37).

How to Apply Shoulder Pads to a T-shirt

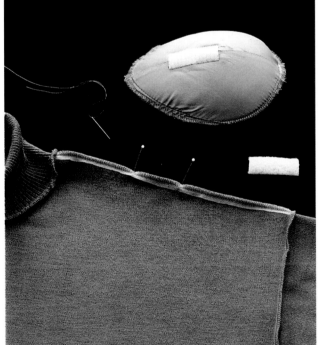

1) Cut two 2" (5 cm) strips of hook and loop tape. Center hook side of tape on shoulder pad; hand-stitch in place. Try on garment, and position shoulder pads as desired, with center of pad at shoulder seam. Pin-mark placement of tape.

2) Center loop side of tape over shoulder seams between markings; stitch tape to seam allowances.

55

Skirts

Knit skirts can range from body-hugging skirts of spandex blends to full skirts of soft, drapable jerseys. Choose the fabric to complement the style of the skirt.

Knit skirts are usually pull-on styles, making them easy to fit and construct. Waistline adjustments are seldom necessary when fitting pull-on styles, and zippers are not required. Pull-on garments are no longer associated only with casual sportswear; dressier skirts also take advantage of this easy construction.

The easiest skirt to sew is a pull-on style with a cut-on waistband (pages 90 to 93); the waistband is simply an extension of the garment sections. Cut-on waistbands are most flattering in slim to moderately full garments.

A variety of looks can be achieved by changing the width of the elastic and by adding topstitching.

To minimize the bulk on fuller styles of skirts, use fabrics that are lighter in weight, or apply a separate waistband (pages 90, 94, and 95), rather than a cut-on waistband. Keep in mind that pull-on skirts must be large enough in the waistline to fit over the fullest part of the hips.

Select the skirt pattern by your hip measurement. The amount of ease required in a skirt depends on the amount of stretch in the fabric and the style of the skirt. If the garment is to have in-seam pockets, allow a minimum of 2" (5 cm) of ease at the hipline to prevent the pockets from gaping.

How to Sew a Pull-on Skirt

1) **Cut** the garment sections, allowing for cut-on waistband as on pages 92 and 93. Or, if a skirt with a separate waistband is desired, cut garment sections and waistband piece as on pages 94 and 95.

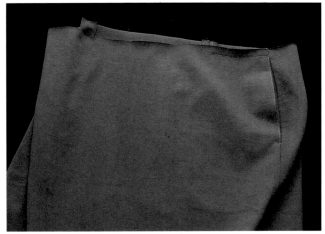

2) **Apply** in-seam pockets (pages 84 and 85), if desired. Stitch side seams.

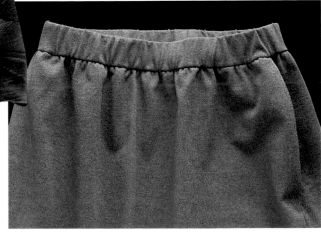

3) **Apply** waistband (pages 92 to 95).

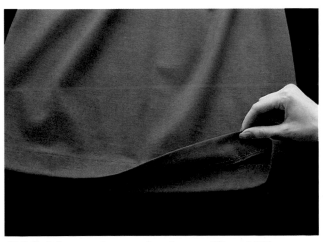

4) **Stitch** hem at lower edge (pages 32 and 33).

Pants & Shorts

Knit pants, usually pull-on styles, take advantage of the fabric's stretch qualities, making them easy to fit and construct. Pull-on pants usually do not need waistline adjustments or time-consuming zipper applications. They vary in style, to include shorts, culottes, capris, and ankle-length pants.

The easiest pants to construct have cut-on waistbands (pages 90 to 93); for sportswear, use drawstring elastic in the waistband, if desired. For styles with more fullness at the waistline, or for the look of a traditional waistband, sew pants with a separate waistband (pages 90, 94, and 95).

Choose pants patterns by your hip measurement. Pull-on pants must be large enough in the waistline to pull over the fullest part of the hips when the fabric is stretched. The amount of ease required depends on the amount of stretch in the fabric and the style of the garment. If the garment is to have in-seam pockets, allow a minimum of 2" (5 cm) of ease at the hipline, to prevent the pockets from gaping. Knit pants do not need as much ease in the crotch depth and crotch length as do woven pants; for a good fit, it is recommended that you use pants patterns designed for knits.

You can line the knee area of knit pants to prevent bagging at the knees. Use a nonfusible knitted interfacing (page 22) or a woven lining fabric, such as batiste.

Pants and shorts can be sewn from knits in a wide variety of styles. The shorts (above) feature a cut-on waistband with drawstring elastic. The culottes (above) have a shirred separate waistband with multiple rows of topstitching, and in-seam pockets. The full-cut pants (opposite) have a separate waistband and in-seam pockets; the shorter capris (opposite) feature a cut-on waistband.

How to Sew Pull-on Pants

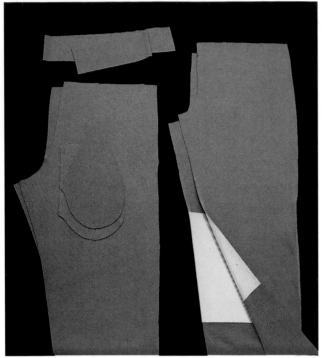

1) Cut pants front and back pieces, allowing for cut-on waistband as on pages 92 and 93. Or, for pants with a separate waistband, cut pants and waistband as on pages 94 and 95. Cut and apply knee lining pieces, if desired (opposite).

2) Apply in-seam pockets (pages 84 and 85), if desired. Stitch side seams.

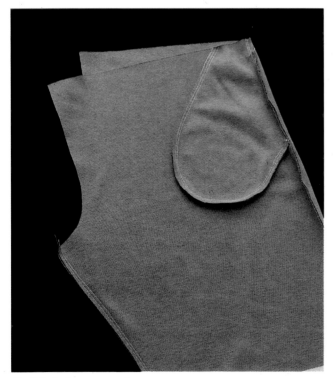

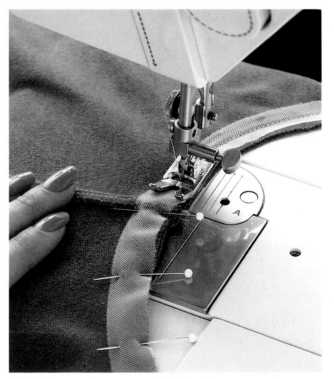

3) Stitch inseams of pants.

4) Stitch crotch seam, stabilizing the seam using tricot bias binding (page 31).

5) **Apply** waistband (pages 92 to 95).

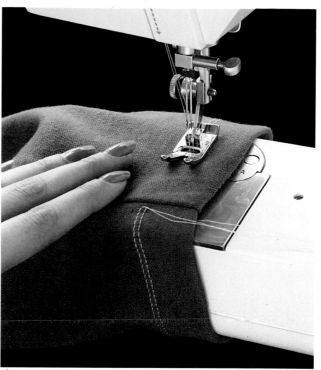

6) **Stitch** hems at the lower edges of the pants legs (pages 32 and 33).

How to Line the Knee Areas of Knit Pants

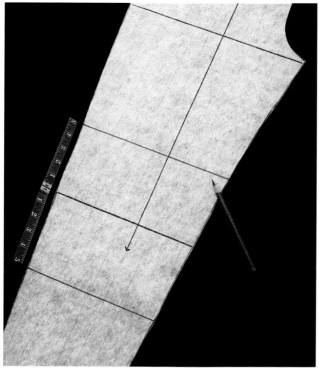

1) **Mark** pants front pattern 5" (12.5 cm) above and below the knee line; use pattern as a guide for cutting lining pieces. If using batiste, finish edges of lining pieces, using overlock stitch or 3-step zigzag stitch.

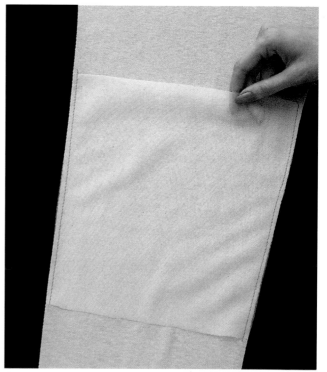

2) **Place** lining on wrong side of pants front in knee area. Baste at inseam and side seam. Lining is stitched in leg seams and remains free at top and bottom.

Cardigans

A cardigan is a classic and versatile addition to a wardrobe. It can coordinate with pants, skirts, and dresses, creating many different ensembles. You may want to make cardigans in long and short styles, varying the type of fabric to make them suitable for either dressy occasions or casual wear.

Select a mediumweight fabric with good body, and select a pattern that has slight curves at the front edges. If the pattern has lower front corners that are squared, you may round them for easier construction.

Apply facings to the cardigan front to help the garment retain its shape and to provide support for the buttons and buttonholes. If a facing piece is not included in the pattern, the facings may be cut using the pattern front as a guide. For added body, apply lightweight interfacing to the fabric before cutting the facings.

An easy way to finish the outer edges of a cardigan is with French binding. With this method, the binding strip is folded in half, resulting in neat, enclosed edges on both the right and the wrong sides. Although French binding is somewhat bulkier than the basic binding on page 42, it has a more finished appearance on the wrong

side of the garment, which is important when the cardigan is worn open.

Choose a lightweight ribbing for the binding to minimize bulk. You may want to use ribbing that is 60" (152.5 cm) wide, or 30" (76 cm) tubular, to eliminate as many seams in the binding as possible.

Cut the French binding strips on the crosswise grain, 3⅝" (9.3 cm) wide and long enough to go around the outer edges of the garment,

including sleeves. Allow extra length for seam allowances and for easing the binding around any outside curves. Piece the strips together as necessary, seaming them diagonally in ¼" (6 mm) seams and lightly pressing the seams open.

Pockets may be added to the cardigan. The upper edges of the pockets are bound, using the basic binding method; cut the pocket binding strips as on page 42.

How to Sew a Cardigan with French Binding

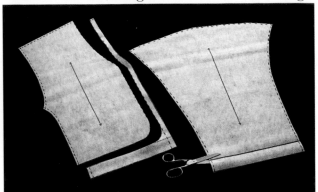

1) Trim seam and hem allowances from pattern front and back pieces at neck, front, and lower edges; round lower corners of pattern front, if necessary. Trim hem allowance from lower edge of sleeve pattern. Remaining seam allowances are ¼" (6 mm).

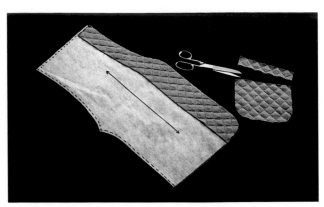

2) Cut garment sections. Cut front facings, using pattern front as a guide, tapering width from 3" (7.5 cm) at lower edge to 2" (5 cm) at shoulder. Cut pockets with ½" (1.3 cm) seam allowances; trim facings from upper edges.

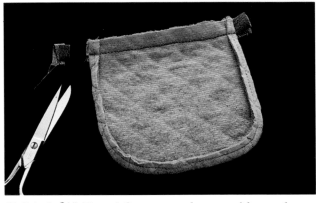

3) Stitch ⅜" (1 cm) from raw edges on sides and lower edge of pocket, stitching each side from upper edge, around corner, to center of lower edge. Press under seam allowances on side and lower edges, pulling up threads at corners to ease in fullness; trim to ¼" (6 mm). Apply pocket binding strips to upper edges and finish ends as on page 45.

4) Apply pocket to garment as on page 82, step 4. Finish long inner edges of facings, if desired; pin facings to garment fronts, wrong sides together. Stitch stabilized shoulder seams (page 31); place tricot bias binding or transparent elastic on garment front. From right side, press seam allowances toward garment back.

5) Press strip for French binding in half lengthwise, wrong sides together. Position strip on lower edge of sleeve, right sides together, matching raw edges; stitch ½" (1.3 cm) seam, stretching binding slightly.

6) Fold binding strip away from sleeve; lightly press seam allowances toward strip. To reduce bulk, trim seam allowances for ⅜" (1 cm) at ends of binding.

7) Fold binding strip around raw edges to wrong side; secure by pinning in the ditch of the seam or with glue stick or liquid basting glue. Stitch along edge of binding from right side, taking care to secure folded edge on wrong side.

8) Stitch sleeves into armholes, right sides together. Stitch one side and sleeve seam, right sides together, starting at lower edge of garment and matching underarm seams; glue-baste binding at seam edges. Lightly press seam allowances toward garment back.

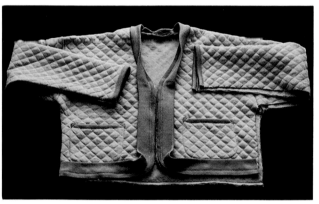

9) Position binding strip around lower, front, and neck edges of garment, right sides together, matching raw edges; stitch ½" (1.3 cm) seam, starting at unstitched side seam. Ease binding at outside curves; stretch binding slightly on lower edge and inner neckline curve. Finish as in steps 6 and 7.

10) Stitch remaining side and sleeve seam; glue-baste binding. Stitch buttonholes in overlap, below; sew buttons to underlap.

How to Sew Buttonholes in Knits

1) Stabilize buttonhole area with pieces of fusible web on both sides; pin in place, but do not fuse. Mark buttonhole placement on fusible web, parallel to ribs of knit. Stitch, lengthening stitch length slightly, if necessary to prevent stretched, uneven buttonhole.

2) Tear away as much fusible web as possible from both sides of garment. Steam remaining fusible web until it disappears, holding iron above, but not on, the fabric.

Easy Design Variations

Design Details

For more variety, several easy design details can be used for knit garments. Quickly and easily change the look of a basic pattern by changing the neckline treatment. Take advantage of the soft hand and drape of knits, and sew cowl and scarf necklines in tops and dresses. Modify a V-necked pullover or add small plackets to the necklines of simple T-shirts.

Add pockets, not just for functional purposes, but for decorative effects as well. Make small pockets and apply them in nontraditional places, such as on sleeves. Or layer one pocket on top of another. Add in-seam pockets to pants and skirts for convenience. Patch pockets can be made inconspicuously from self-fabric and hemmed, or become the focal point of a garment when sewn in contrasting fabric or trimmed with ribbing. Window pockets make fun-and-easy design details. Make welt pockets that look difficult to sew, but are an easy adaptation of the window pocket.

The waistband, an important part of any skirt or pants, can be both functional and attractive. Choose an elasticized waistband for easy sewing and a comfortable fit. The waistband can be "cut on" for faster cutting and sewing, or cut as a separate piece. When finished, it can look like a traditional, smooth waistband or one that is shirred.

For a look that is unique, sew layered and slashed knit garments, creating a wearable work of art. Or simply add a twisted knit trim to creatively embellish a garment.

Necklines may have softly draped cowl or scarf collars or tailored details like plackets and bindings.

Pockets add interest to basic knit garments. Embellished with topstitching or trimmed with ribbing, they are decorative as well as functional.

Elasticized waistbands are especially suitable for knits. Easy to sew as well as comfortable, they come in several styles.

Decorative effects, like layered and slashed fabrics and twisted trims, add surface interest to garments.

69

Cowl Necklines

Cowl necklines, which create softly draped fabric, are especially appropriate for knits. Select knits that are soft and lightweight, such as single knit, interlock, or lightweight ribbing.

Two popular styles are the traditional cowl (left) and the shifted cowl (right). The traditional cowl can be arranged in defined, regular folds, while the shifted cowl has an irregular, crushed look with soft folds.

How to Sew a Traditional Cowl Neckline

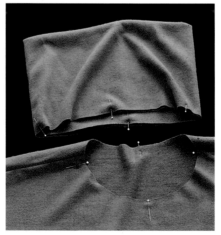

1) Stitch short ends of cowl piece, right sides together, forming a circle; press seam. Fold cowl, wrong sides together, matching raw edges and seamline.

2) Divide cowl into fourths; pin-mark, with one pin at seamline. Divide neck edge into fourths; pin-mark, with one pin at center back.

3) Place cowl on the right side of garment, matching raw edges and pin marks, with seamline at center back. Stitch the neckline seam.

70

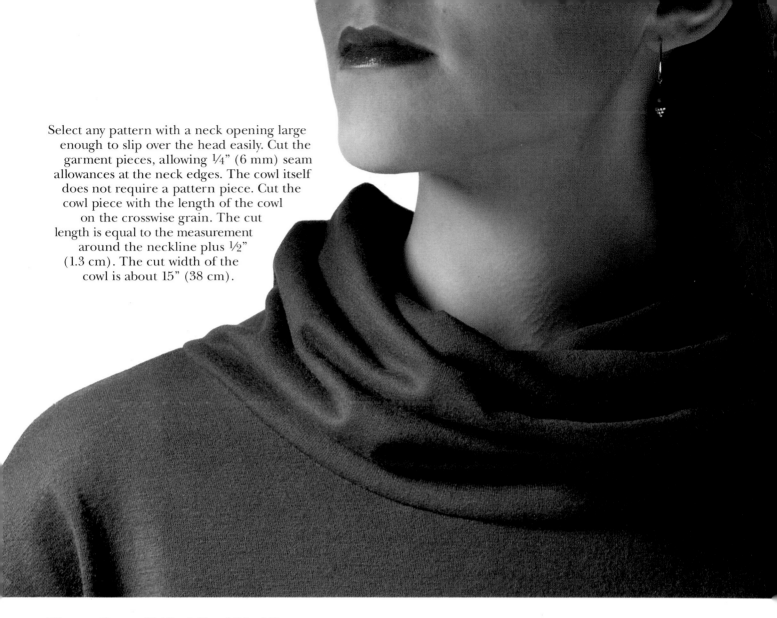

Select any pattern with a neck opening large enough to slip over the head easily. Cut the garment pieces, allowing ¼" (6 mm) seam allowances at the neck edges. The cowl itself does not require a pattern piece. Cut the cowl piece with the length of the cowl on the crosswise grain. The cut length is equal to the measurement around the neckline plus ½" (1.3 cm). The cut width of the cowl is about 15" (38 cm).

How to Sew a Shifted Cowl Neckline

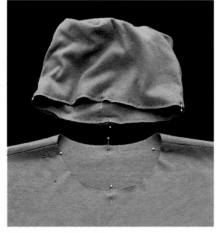

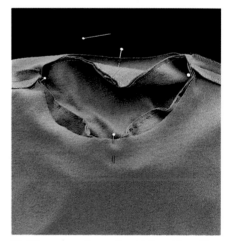

1) Stitch short ends of cowl piece, right sides together, forming a circle; press seam. Fold cowl, wrong sides together, matching raw edges; shift fabric layers horizontally so seamline is offset 4" (10 cm) at raw edges.

2) Baste shifted layers together a scant ¼" (6 mm) from raw edges. Place pin at seamline on one side of cowl to mark center back. Divide cowl into fourths; pin-mark. Divide neck edge into fourths; pin-mark.

3) Place cowl on the right side of garment, matching raw edges and pin marks, with seamline at center back against garment. Stitch the neckline seam.

Scarf Necklines

Scarf necklines have a draped cowl-like collar that is attached to the garment in the back and hangs free in the front. The collar may be cut to any length and width desired.

Choose a pattern with a neckline that fits over your head easily. Choose a soft, drapable fabric, such as jersey, interlock, or a lightweight sweater knit. When selecting a fabric, also consider that the wrong side of the fabric may show during wear.

Determine the dimensions to cut the collar by draping a rectangle of fabric, as shown opposite. Start with a rectangle the width of the yardage by 13" to 15" (33 to 38 cm).

How to Sew a Scarf Neckline

1) **Cut** garment pieces, allowing ½" (1.3 cm) seam allowances at neck edge. Construct garment, finishing neck edge using the turned-and-stitched edge finish, as on page 51.

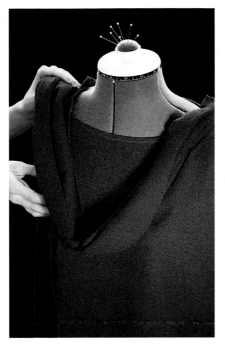

2) **Pin** collar to garment at shoulder seams, draping collar in front neckline; adjust length of drape for desired look.

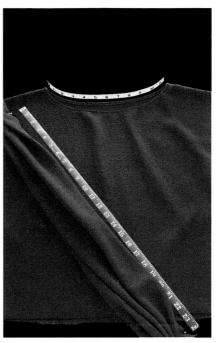

3) **Measure** draped length between shoulder seams. Cut collar to a length equal to this measurement plus the garment back neck edge measurement plus 1" (2.5 cm) for seam allowances.

4) **Stitch** ½" (1.3 cm) center back seam on collar. Press seam allowances to one side. Topstitch ¼" (6 mm) from seamline through all layers; trim seam allowances close to stitching.

5) **Press** under ⅝" (1.5 cm) on raw edges of collar. Fold raw edges under again to meet first fold; press. Topstitch hems in place.

6) **Lap** one hemmed edge of collar over garment back neckline, with wrong side of collar to right side of garment, matching topstitching lines and center backs; pin. Stitch over previous topstitching lines between the shoulder seams.

Modified V Necks

Sew this pullover with a modified V neck, starting with a typical V-neck pattern designed for ribbing. Straighten the neckline opening at the center front, and apply the ribbing, using a lapped method. The right side of the ribbing is lapped over the left side for women's garments, or the left side over the right for men's garments.

How to Apply Lapped Ribbing to a Modified V Neckline

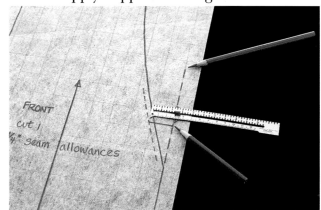

1) **Extend** center front line of pattern. Draw horizontal seamline on pattern, from center front to seamline, at point where distance equals one-half the finished width of ribbing. Cut garment pieces, using adjusted pattern; allow ¼" (6 mm) seam allowances at neckline.

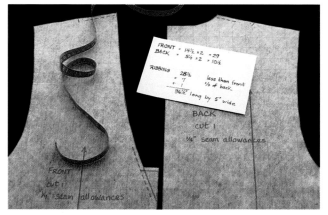

2) **Measure** front and back necklines on pattern, from shoulder seams to center lines; multiply each measurement by two. Cut ribbing slightly shorter than front neckline plus two-thirds of back neckline plus 1" (2.5 cm). Cut ribbing to width specified by pattern, allowing ¼" (6 mm) seam allowances.

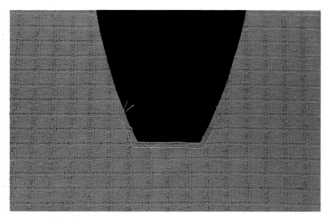

3) Reinforce corners of front neckline by staystitching scant ¼" (6 mm) from raw edge, using short straight stitches. Stitch shoulder seams.

4) Fold ribbing in half lengthwise; pin to right side of front neckline, matching raw edges, with one end of ribbing extending beyond corner an amount equal to finished width. Stitch ¼" (6 mm) seam from staystitching at corner to first shoulder seam, stretching ribbing slightly.

5) Lift presser foot, leaving needle down at shoulder seam. On ribbing, measure from needle a distance equal to two-thirds of back neckline; pin-mark.

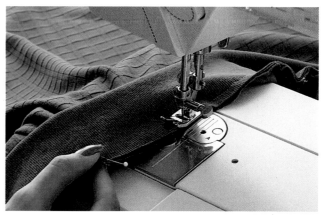

6) Match pin mark to the remaining shoulder seam. Stretch ribbing, and stitch to back neckline. Continue stitching along remaining front neckline to staystitching at corner, stretching ribbing slightly.

7) Clip garment fabric to, but not through, staystitched corners. Lightly press seam allowances toward garment. From right side, fold under horizontal seam allowance; pin ribbing at center front in lapped position. (Woman's garment is shown.)

8) Fold garment front up, exposing horizontal seam allowance. Adjust lapped ribbing as necessary, so folded edges are at corners; pin or glue-baste in place. Stitch horizontal seam; trim excess ribbing. Finish raw edges, if desired, using overlock stitch.

Plackets

Duplicate the look of women's ready-to-wear by adding a narrow placket to T-shirts and tank tops. Then finish the necklines of the garments with a ribbed edge (page 35) or narrow binding (page 42).

These instructions are for plackets with a finished width of ¾" (2 cm), but they may be sewn in any length. You may want to add a 3" (7.5 cm) placket to a tank top or crewneck T-shirt. Or embellish the scoop neckline of a T-shirt with an 8" (20.5 cm) placket and decorative buttons or snaps.

The placket facings may be cut from self-fabric or coordinating fabric. Apply interfacing to the fabric for added body, if necessary (page 22). For plackets on heavier knit shirts, use a coordinating fabric that is lighter in weight to reduce bulk. For the decorative look of piping, a contrasting facing may be rolled to the outside of the garment on the overlap side of the placket.

The plackets of women's garments lap right over left, so the placket opening is marked on the left side of the center front, as shown in step 2, opposite. As you work through the following steps, keep in mind that "left" and "right" refer to the left and right sides of the garment as it will be worn.

How to Sew a Placket with a Bound Neckline

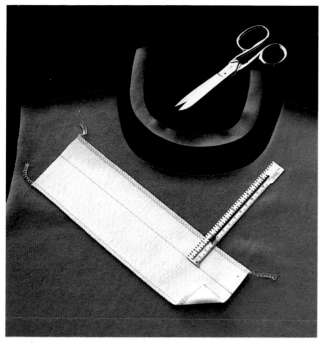

1) Cut garment pieces; trim seam allowances from neck edges. Cut placket facing from interfaced fabric to desired finished length of placket opening plus 2" (5 cm); the cut width is 3¼" (8.2 cm). Overlock long edges of facing, if desired. Mark a line on the facing, on right side of fabric, 1¼" (3.2 cm) from one long edge.

2) Mark center front of garment with dotted line on right side of fabric; mark placket opening with solid line to desired finished length, ½" (1.3 cm) to the left of center front. Cut on solid line.

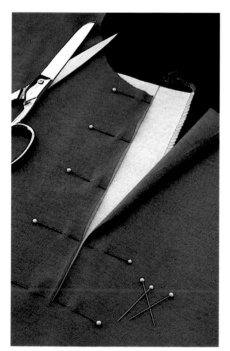

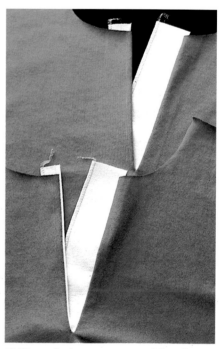

3) Pin facing to garment, right sides together, with upper edge of facing ½" (1.3 cm) above neck edge and with marked line on facing directly under placket opening. Narrow side of facing is placed to the right of center front.

4) Stitch around placket opening of garment, ⅛" (3 mm) from raw edges, using a short stitch length. Taper stitches at bottom of opening, and make one stitch across point of slash. Cut facing on marked line.

5) Turn facing to wrong side of the garment. Press facing on overlap side, rolling seam slightly to the underside (top). Or for a piped effect, press a fold in the facing on overlap side, with the placket seam about ⅛" (3 mm) from fold (bottom).

(Continued on next page)

6) Press underlap seam allowances toward facing. Press a fold in facing on underlap side, wrong sides together, with fold ¾" (2 cm) from placket opening seam. Trim facing to match neckline curve.

7) Stitch in the ditch or edgestitch the underlap in place. If desired, topstitch the overlap, through all layers, from upper to lower edge of placket, with stitching ¾" (2 cm) from seamline.

8) Stitch a narrow rectangle across width of placket at lower end, stitching through all layers. From the wrong side, trim excess fabric at lower end of facing. Make buttonholes (page 65) on overlap; attach buttons to underlap.

9) Stitch shoulder seams. Apply binding and finish the ends as on page 45, steps 1 to 3.

How to Sew a Placket with a Ribbed Neckline

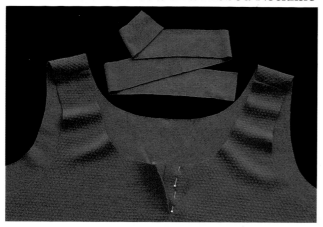

1) Cut garment pieces, allowing ¼" (6 mm) seam allowances at neck edge. Follow steps 1 to 6 on pages 77 and 78. Stitch shoulder seams. Measure neckline, including underlap. Cut length of ribbing to two-thirds of neckline measurement plus ½" (1.3 cm); the cut width of the ribbing is 2" (5 cm).

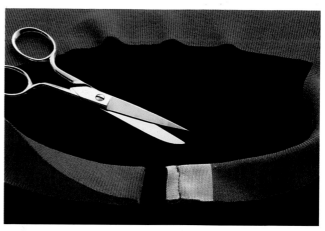

2) Apply 1" (2.5 cm) strip of fusible interfacing to ends of ribbing; do not stretch ribbing. Fold ends of ribbing in half lengthwise, right sides together. Stitch ¼" (6 mm) seams across ends of ribbing; trim. Fold right side out; press ends lightly.

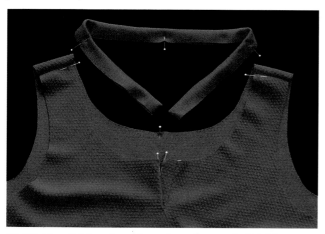

3) Divide ribbing into fourths; pin-mark. Divide neckline opening into fourths, beginning and ending at folded edges; pin-mark.

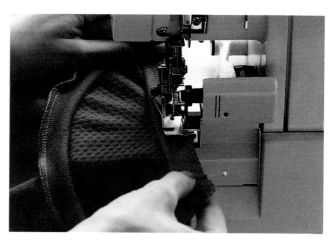

4) Pin ribbing to garment, with right sides together and raw edges even, matching pin marks; stitch.

5) Fold facings over ribbing, right sides together; pin. Stitch along upper edge of facings, over previous stitching; trim corners and grade seam allowances.

6) Turn facings to wrong side of garment; press seam allowances toward garment. Finish placket, following steps 7 and 8, opposite.

Patch Pockets

Patch pockets are a quick detail that can be added to a garment without using a pattern piece. Hemmed at the upper edge or trimmed with ribbing, they are a versatile and popular pocket style.

To create perfect pockets without stretching the knit fabric, the pocket pieces are staystitched. Then, to keep the fabric from shifting as the pocket is applied, it is glue-basted to the garment, using glue stick or liquid basting glue.

To prevent the upper edge of a hemmed knit pocket from sagging, the hem allowance is stabilized with fusible interfacing. To prevent sagging on a ribbed-edge pocket, the ribbing is cut slightly shorter than the upper edge.

For a hemmed pocket, cut the pocket piece from fabric 1" (2.5 cm) wider than the desired finished width of the pocket, to allow for ½" (1.3 cm) seam

allowances. Cut the pocket 1¼" to 1½" (3.2 to 3.8 cm) longer than the desired finished length, to allow for a ½" (1.3 cm) seam allowance at the lower edge and a ¾" to 1" (2 to 2.5 cm) hem allowance at the upper edge. Round the lower corners of the pocket piece, if desired.

For a ribbed-edge pocket with 1" (2.5 cm) finished ribbing, cut the pocket piece from fabric 1" (2.5 cm) wider than the desired finished width of the pocket, to allow for ½" (1.3 cm) seam allowances. Cut the pocket ¼" (6 mm) shorter than the desired finished length, allowing for ½" (1.3 cm) seam allowance at the lower edge and ¼" (6 mm) seam allowance at the ribbed upper edge. Round the lower corners, if desired. From ribbing, cut a piece ½" (1.3 cm) shorter than the cut width of the pocket piece and 2½" (6.5 cm) wide, with the crosswise grain of the ribbing along the pocket width.

Tips for Perfect Patch Pockets

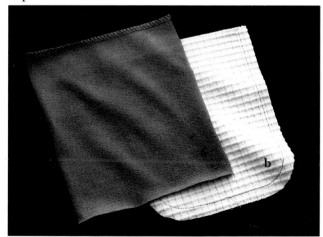

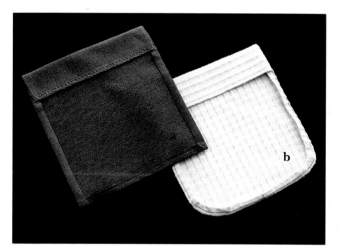

Staystitch ⅜" (1 cm) from edges. For pockets with square corners, staystitch along lower edge **(a).** For pockets with round corners, staystitch along sides and lower edge; starting at upper corner, stitch down side of pocket, around lower corner, to center of lower edge **(b).**

Make perfect corners on pockets with square corners **(a)** by glue-basting trimmed seam allowances together; or, on pockets with round corners **(b),** by pulling staystitching threads to ease in fullness at corners.

Pocket with square corners. 1) Cut lightweight interfacing the width of pocket and ¼" (6 mm) deeper than hem of pocket; fuse to wrong side of pocket at upper edge. Finish upper edge of pocket, if desired. Staystitch pocket (page 81).

2) Fold hem allowance to right side of pocket. On each side, pull raw edge of hem allowance ⅛" (3 mm) beyond raw edge of pocket. Stitch seams ½" (1.3 cm) from raw edge of hem allowance; trim and grade seams at hem. Turn right side out.

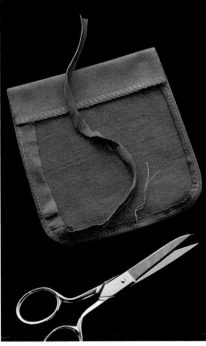

3) Press under seam allowances on sides and lower edge. Trim lower corners diagonally; trim seam allowances to ¼" (6 mm). Glue-baste lower corners (page 81).

4) Topstitch hem in place from right side. Apply glue stick to seam allowances on the sides and lower edge; position pocket on garment. Edgestitch around the pocket, reinforcing upper corners as shown.

Pocket with round corners. Follow steps 1 and 2, above. Press under seam allowances at sides and lower edge, pulling up threads at corners to ease in fullness. Trim seam allowances to ¼" (6 mm). Finish as in step 4.

How to Sew a Patch Pocket with Ribbing

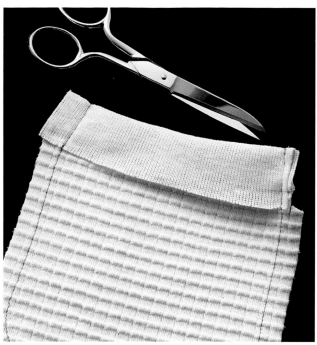

1) Staystitch pocket (page 81). Press ribbing in half lengthwise, wrong sides together. Place ribbing on pocket, right sides together, matching one edge of ribbing to upper edge of pocket. Stitch ¼" (6 mm) seam, stretching ribbing to fit. Lightly press seam allowances toward ribbing.

2) Fold ribbing to right side of pocket along pressed foldline. Pull raw edge of ribbing facing ⅛" (3 mm) beyond raw edge of pocket. Stitch seams ½" (1.3 cm) from raw edges of facing. Trim and grade seam allowances at sides of ribbing; turn right side out.

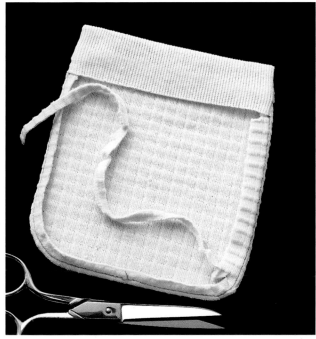

3) Press under seam allowances at sides and lower edge. For pocket with rounded corners, pull up threads at corners to ease in fullness; for pocket with square corners, trim lower corners diagonally. Trim seam allowances to ¼" (6 mm). Glue-baste lower corners (page 81).

4) Stitch in the ditch from right side to secure the ribbing edge. Apply glue stick to seam allowances on sides and lower edge; position pocket on garment, stretching ribbing slightly for straight sides. Edgestitch around pocket, reinforcing upper corners as shown.

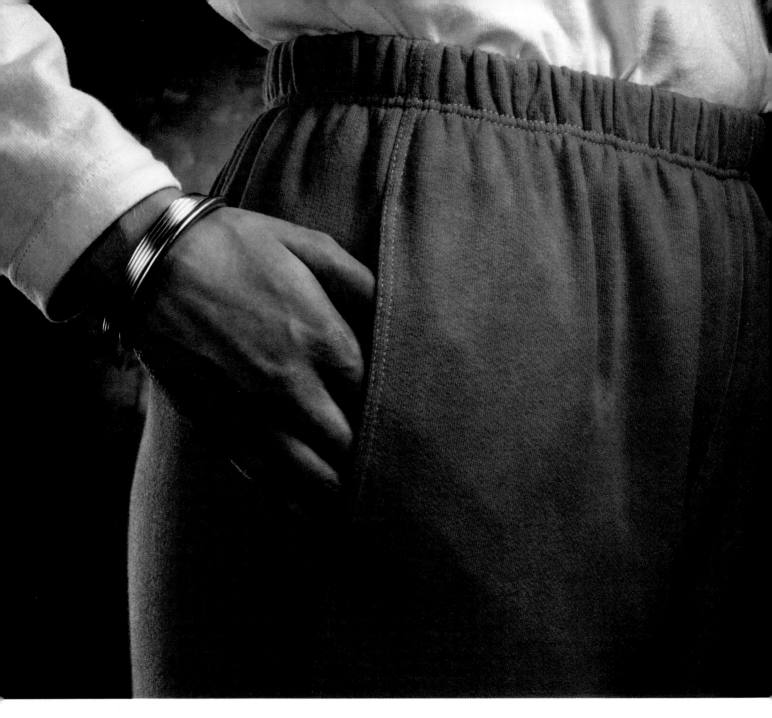

In-seam Pockets

In-seam pockets are quick and easy to make. The method shown here is similar to that used by ready-to-wear manufacturers. This technique may be used with patterns that have ¼" (6 mm) or ⅝" (1.5 cm) seam allowances; the seam allowances may be either pressed open or pressed toward the garment back.

When sewn from two layers of garment fabric, in-seam pockets can sometimes be bulky. To reduce bulk, a lightweight fabric, such as nonfusible knitted interfacing, may be used for the pocket facing. Because this type of interfacing has a soft hand and does not ravel, it is especially compatible with knits.

Used as the pocket facing, it stabilizes the pocket edge and helps the pocket stay flat. Before cutting the interfacing, preshrink it by laundering or steam pressing.

Since nonfusible knitted interfacing is available in a limited number of colors, select the one closest to the color of the garment fabric. You may use a lightweight batiste, broadcloth, or stable tricot lining of a matching color instead, or use the garment fabric if it is lightweight; cut the pocket facing with the pocket opening on the straight of grain.

How to Sew an In-seam Pocket

1) Mark pocket opening on the pocket facing and the garment front. Place pocket facing on garment, right sides together, matching marked lines.

2) Stitch from raw edge to end of pocket opening, using short stitches. Pivot at seamline and stitch to other end of opening; pivot and stitch to raw edge. At corners, clip seam allowances at an angle to, but not through, the stitching. Trim 5/8" (1.5 cm) seam allowances to 1/4" (6 mm) at pocket opening.

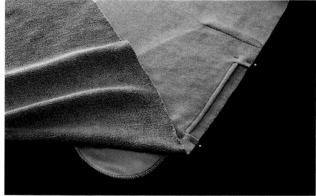

3) Turn pocket facing to wrong side of garment front; press, with seamline rolled slightly to the facing side. With pocket facing extended, understitch along pocket opening next to seamline.

4) Fold pocket facing and garment front wrong sides together. Edgestitch or topstitch around pocket opening, stitching through all layers.

5) Align pocket back to pocket facing, right sides together; pin. Overlock or double-stitch around curved outer edge of pocket through both layers. For pocket on skirt or pants, machine-baste pocket in place at waistline seam.

6) Machine-baste pocket to garment section at side seam, stitching from right side of garment. Place garment front and garment back right sides together; pin. Stitch side seam, taking care not to catch pocket opening in stitching. Press 1/4" (6 mm) seam allowances toward garment back, or press 5/8" (1.5 cm) seam allowances open.

Window Pockets

Add a window pocket as an interesting detail on knit garments. This decorative pocket works well as a breast pocket on a T-shirt or in the hip area of a cardigan. Accent the pocket by stitching around the pocket opening with a single, double, or triple needle; this stitching also helps keep the opening flat. A button-and-loop detail can be added to keep larger pockets from gaping open.

The instructions shown here are for a pocket opening ⅜" (1 cm) wide. The length of the opening may be any size desired. To eliminate bulk, use nonfusible

knitted interfacing (page 22) for the pocket facing and garment fabric for the pocket back. Contrasting fabric may be used for the pocket back to emphasize the pocket opening, if desired.

Determine the desired position of the pocket, and mark the ends and center line of the opening on the right side of the garment section. On the lengthwise grain, cut one rectangle of interfacing and one of garment fabric, each 6" (15 cm) long by the width of the pocket opening plus 1½" (3.8 cm).

How to Sew a Window Pocket

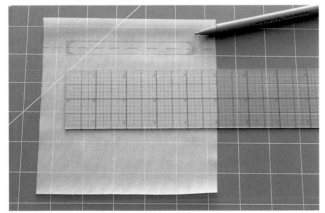

1) Draw a dotted line on pocket facing, on the crosswise grain, 1" (2.5 cm) from upper edge. Draw rectangle, centered on this line, ⅜" (1 cm) wide by length of pocket opening. Round the corners of the rectangle if you intend to topstitch with a double or triple needle.

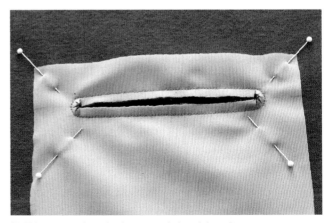

2) Place pocket facing on right side of garment section, matching center lines; pin in place. Stitch around rectangle on marked lines, using short straight stitches. Slash through pocket facing and garment section on center line, then diagonally to, but not through, corners.

3) Press flat. Turn facing to wrong side; press with seamline rolled slightly to the facing side.

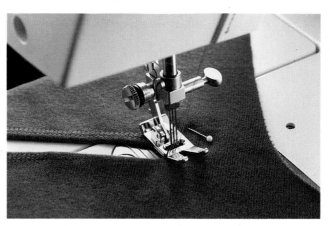

4) Edgestitch around pocket opening. If using double or triple needle, turn flywheel by hand at curves, lifting presser foot with needles down and turning garment slightly after each stitch.

5) Fold garment up, exposing pocket facing. Place pocket back piece under facing; pin in place. Mark stitching line next to pocket ends and around the bottom, curving corners.

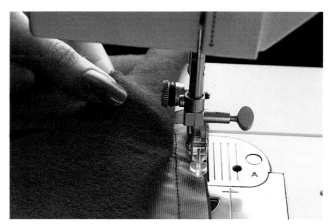

6) Stitch as close as possible to top of pocket opening, using zipper foot. Continue on marked line. Stitch again ¼" (6 mm) away from first row of stitching. Trim both layers next to stitching.

How to Make a Window Pocket with a Button Loop

1) Cut ¾" × 4" (2 × 10 cm) fabric strip for button loop. Fold strip into thirds lengthwise; press. Topstitch through center of strip, stretching strip as you sew. Trim raw edge close to stitching on back of button loop. Follow steps 1 to 5, opposite, for window pocket.

2) Fold fabric strip to form loop; place between pocket facing and pocket back piece at upper edge of pocket. Pin loop in place, adjusting size of loop to fit button. Follow step 6, catching button loop in stitching. Attach button at lower edge of pocket, stitching through garment and pocket facing.

Welt Pockets

Add welt pockets to a garment for a classic look of quality. Welt pockets are suitable for sportswear as well as for more tailored knit styles. Although welt pockets may look difficult, this welt pocket is very easy to construct. The window pocket (pages 86 and 87) is transformed into a single welt pocket by adjusting its size and shape, then inserting a welt made from ribbing or self-fabric.

The instructions shown here are for a pocket with a finished welt that measures 1" × 5" (2.5 × 12.5 cm). Use garment fabric for the pocket back, but to

eliminate bulk, use nonfusible knitted interfacing (page 22) for the pocket facing.

Determine the desired position of the pocket, and mark the ends and center line of the opening on the right side of the garment section. Cut a fabric strip for the welt, 6" (15 cm) wide, on the crosswise grain, by 3" (7.5 cm) long; if self-fabric is used for the welt, apply interfacing. Cut one 6½" (16.3 cm) square from garment fabric and one from nonfusible knitted interfacing for the pocket.

How to Sew a Welt Pocket

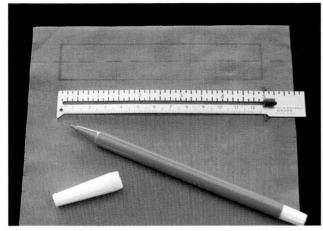

1) **Draw** a dotted line on interfacing piece, on the crosswise grain, 1" (2.5 cm) from upper edge. Draw 1" × 5" (2.5 × 12.5 cm) rectangle, centered on the dotted line. Construct opening for welt, as on pages 86 and 87, steps 2 and 3.

2) **Fold** fabric strip for welt in half lengthwise, wrong sides together and raw edges even; press. Secure raw edges, using glue stick or liquid basting glue.

3) **Apply** glue stick or liquid basting glue along lower edge on wrong side of pocket opening. Center the fabric strip on opening with folded edge even with upper edge of opening; finger-press edge of opening.

4) **Fold** garment up to expose pocket facing, and stitch, using zipper foot, next to previous stitching on ends and lower edge of opening. Trim seam allowances.

5) **Turn** to opposite side, and zigzag raw edges of the welt to pocket facing.

6) **Complete** welt pocket as for window pocket on page 87, steps 5 and 6.

Elasticized Waistbands

Elasticized waistbands are comfortable to wear and easy to sew. They complement the stretch of knit fabrics. Some elasticized waistbands are "cut on," while others are a separate waistband piece. Choose an application technique according to the fabric, the garment style, and the type of elastic you are using (page 22).

Two techniques for cut-on waistbands are included: cut-on waistbands with casings and cut-on waistbands with topstitching. For both techniques, the waistbands are cut as an extension of the garment at the waistline edge. Cut-on waistbands are appropriate for garments made from lightweight to mediumweight fabrics.

Cut-on waistbands with casings (a) give a casual look. Firm braided or woven elastics are well suited for this technique. Because the elastic is not caught in the waistline seam, it can easily be adjusted for a better fit, if necessary.

Cut-on waistbands with topstitching (b) give a variety of looks, depending on the type of topstitching. Use an elastic with good stretch and recovery qualities so the elastic will stretch to the circumference of the garment opening, yet retain its fit. Drawstring elastic (c) may be used for this method.

Two additional techniques are included for waistbands that use a separate waistband piece: smooth waistbands and shirred waistbands. When sewing garments from lightweight or mediumweight knits, you may cut the waistband from self-fabric. When sewing bulky fabrics, such as sweatshirt fleece, choose matching ribbing for the waistband or, for a more decorative effect, a contrasting fabric.

Smooth separate waistbands (d) give the smooth appearance of a traditional waistband when the garment is worn. This waistband style is suitable for a slim-fitting garment made from lightweight or mediumweight knit fabric with moderate stretch. Use a firm 1" or 1¼" (2.5 or 3.2 cm) elastic.

Shirred separate waistbands (e) complement fuller garment styles, such as full skirts, and are especially attractive when used with wider elastics. Shirred waistbands may be topstitched or not, depending on the look you prefer. Firm elastic is recommended for this type of waistband.

In general, cut elastics 2" to 3" (5 to 7.5 cm) less than your waist measurement. Cut soft, lightweight elastics, such as knit elastics, 3" to 5" (7.5 to 12.5 cm) less than your waist measurement. Cut very firm elastics, such as nonroll waistband elastic, equal to, or 1" (2.5 cm) less than, your waist measurement. Mark the elastic, and pin it around your waistline before cutting it. Check to see that the elastic fits comfortably around your waist and pulls over your hips easily.

Multiple rows of topstitching can cause elastic to lose some of its recovery. If you are using a method that calls for topstitching, you may want to cut the elastic up to 1" (2.5 cm) shorter than the guidelines, to ensure a snug fit.

Tips for Sewing Elasticized Waistbands

Preshrink elastics for casing applications before measuring. Elastics that will be stitched on do not require preshrinking.

Use longer stitches, about 8 to 9 stitches per inch (2.5 cm), when stitching through the elastic; the stitches will appear shorter when elastic is relaxed. A stitch length that is too short weakens and stretches out the elastic.

Steam the finished waistband after construction, holding the iron above the fabric, to help the elastic return to its original length.

Two Ways to Join the Ends of the Elastic

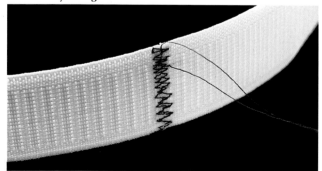

Butted method. Butt ends of elastic. Stitch back and forth, using 3-step zigzag stitch or wide zigzag stitch, catching both ends of elastic in stitching. This method is recommended for firm elastics.

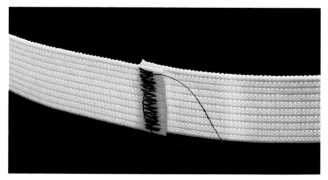

Overlapped method. Overlap ends of elastic ½" (1.3 cm). Stitch back and forth through both layers, using wide zigzag stitch or 3-step zigzag stitch. Use for soft elastics, such as knitted elastic.

How to Sew a Cut-on Waistband with a Casing

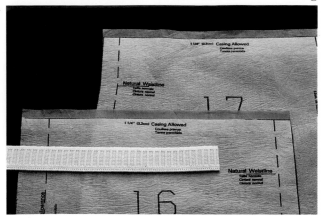

1) **Extend** garment pattern pieces above waistline twice the width of the elastic plus 5/8" (1.5 cm). Cut out garment sections, and stitch together.

2) **Overlock** raw edge at waist, if desired. Fold edge of fabric to wrong side, an amount equal to width of elastic plus 1/2" (1.3 cm). Edgestitch close to fold.

3) **Join** ends of elastic (page 90). Position elastic within folded casing area. Stitch next to elastic, using straight stitch and zipper foot; do not catch elastic in stitching. Shift fabric around elastic as necessary while stitching.

4) **Stretch** waistband to distribute fabric evenly. From right side of garment, stitch in the ditch through all waistband layers, at center front, center back, and side seams, to secure elastic.

Alternate method. 1) Follow steps 1 and 2, above. Mark elastic to desired length; do not cut. Position elastic within folded casing area. Stitch next to elastic, using straight stitch and zipper foot, leaving 2" (5 cm) unstitched; do not catch elastic in stitching.

2) **Pull** elastic through to marking; secure, using safety pin. Try on garment to check fit; adjust elastic, if necessary. Cut and join ends of elastic (page 90). Complete waistband stitching. Stitch in the ditch as in step 4, above.

How to Sew a Cut-on Waistband with Topstitching

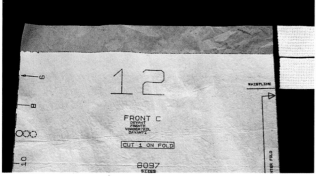

1) **Extend** garment pattern pieces above waistline twice the width of the elastic. Cut out garment sections, and stitch together. Join ends of elastic (page 90).

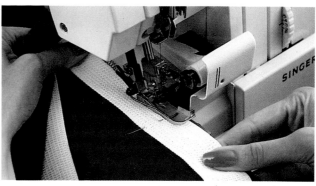

2) **Divide** elastic and garment edge into fourths; pin-mark. Pin elastic to wrong side of garment, with edges even, matching pin marks; overlock or zigzag, stretching elastic to fit between pins. If using overlock machine, guide work carefully or disengage knives to avoid cutting elastic.

3) **Fold** elastic to wrong side of garment so fabric encases elastic. From right side of garment, stitch in the ditch through all waistband layers, at center front, center back, and side seams, to secure elastic.

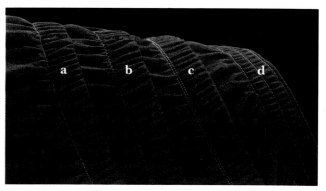

4) **Topstitch** through all layers of waistband, stretching elastic as you sew. Straight-stitch or narrow zigzag close to lower edge of casing, using long stitches (**a**); zigzag close to lower edge, using medium-to-wide stitches (**b**); double-needle topstitch close to lower edge (**c**); or stitch three or more evenly spaced rows of straight stitching or double-needle stitching (**d**).

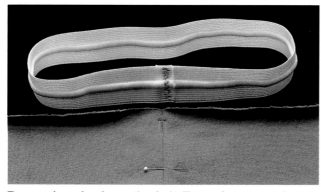

Drawstring-elastic method. 1) Extend pattern pieces as in step 1, above. Join ends of drawstring elastic, using overlapped method (page 90). Stitch garment sections together, leaving ½" (1.3 cm) opening in center front seam in drawstring area; topstitch around opening to secure.

2) **Follow** step 2, above. Stitch again at lower edge of elastic, using zigzag stitch. Fold elastic to wrong side of garment so fabric encases elastic. Stitch ¼" (6 mm) from upper and lower edges of elastic, through all layers, using straight stitch and stretching elastic to fit. Pull drawstring through center front opening. Cut drawstring, and knot ends.

How to Sew a Smooth Separate Waistband

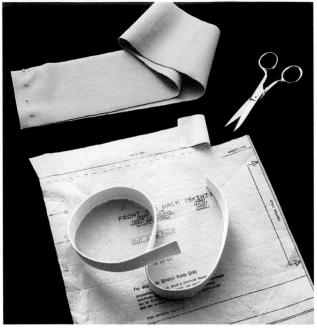

1) **Mark** cutting line on garment section pattern pieces ⅝" (1.5 cm) above waistline. Cut waistband on crosswise grain, twice the width of elastic plus 1¼" (3.2 cm); length of waistband is equal to your waist measurement plus 3¼" (8.2 cm). Pin ends of waistband together with ⅝" (1.5 cm) seam allowances; check fit over hips.

2) **Join** ends of waistband; press seam open. Divide waistband and garment edge into fourths; pin-mark. Pin waistband to right side of garment, with raw edges even, matching pin marks. Stitch ⅝" (1.5 cm) seam, using straight stitch or narrow zigzag stitch; if using straight stitch, stretch fabric as you sew.

3) **Join** ends of elastic (page 90). Divide elastic and garment edge into fourths; pin-mark. Place elastic on seam allowance of waistband; pin in place, with lower edge of elastic just above seamline. With elastic on top, stitch through both seam allowances, using wide zigzag or multiple zigzag stitch; stretch elastic to fit between pins. Trim seam allowances.

4) **Fold** waistband tightly over elastic to wrong side of garment; pin. Stitch in the ditch along seamline from right side of garment, stretching elastic; catch waistband in stitching on wrong side of garment, but do not catch elastic. Trim waistband seam allowance to ¼" (6 mm) from stitching.

How to Sew a Shirred Separate Waistband

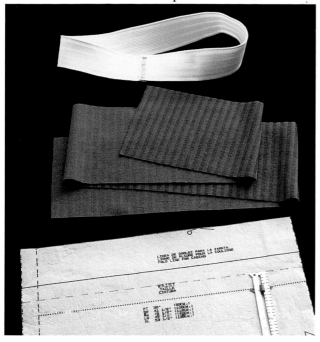

1) **Mark** cutting line on garment section pattern pieces ⅝" (1.5 cm) above waistline. Cut waistband on crosswise grain, twice the width of elastic plus 1¼" (3.2 cm); length of waistband is equal to your hip measurement plus 1¼" (3.2 cm). Join ends of elastic (page 90).

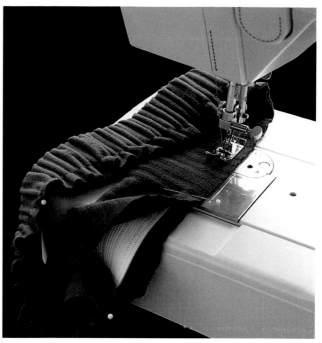

2) **Join** ends of waistband in ⅝" (1.5 cm) seam; press seam open. Divide the waistband and garment edges into fourths; pin-mark. Fold the waistband in half lengthwise, wrong sides together, encasing elastic. Baste ½" (1.3 cm) from raw edges, avoiding pins; shift fabric around elastic as necessary.

3) **Pin** waistband to right side of garment, matching pin marks; if garment is very full, gather waistline edge before attaching waistband. Stitch just inside basting stitches, stretching waistband to fit garment between pins. Trim seam allowances to ¼" (6 mm). Overlock raw edges, if desired.

4) **Stretch** waistband to distribute fabric evenly. From right side of garment, stitch perpendicular to the waistline through all waistband layers, at the center back and side seams, to secure the elastic. If desired, topstitch through all layers as on page 93, step 4.

Layered & Slashed Garments

Single-knit fabric curls at the edges to create an interesting, tubelike effect.

Layering and slashing knit fabrics gives a textured, decorative effect to knit garments. Several layers of fabric are stitched together in rows and slashed midway between the rows, causing the fabric to curl, or "bloom." If desired, you may then stitch across the slashed layers, creating an overall pattern. After the garment is washed and dried by machine once or twice, the raw edges of the knit layers curl even more, adding dimension and interest.

Lightweight to mediumweight knits of 100 percent cotton or cotton blends are used to achieve the curled effect; do not prewash the fabrics. Avoid knits of 100 percent polyester.

Double-knit fabrics, such as cotton interlocks, work well for most designs. Single-knit fabrics may be used; their tendency to curl toward the wrong side on the lengthwise grain can create interesting tubelike effects (top right). If single-knit fabric is placed right side down, then slashed on the lengthwise grain, the edges curl up.

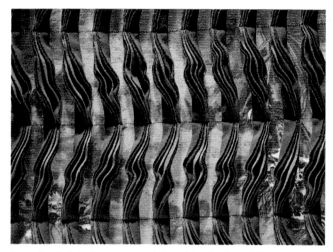

Interlock fabric was used for this design. The rows of stitching were added across the slashes at 4" (10 cm) intervals, changing the direction of the slashed edges.

Choose the fabric types and colors based on the design you want to achieve. Depending on the design, the top, bottom, or any of the middle layers may become the dominant fabric in the finished garment. Test the fabrics, sequences for layering, and designs by sewing samples 12" × 14" (30.5 × 35.5 cm) or larger before cutting out the garment. Be sure to wash and dry the samples at least once to see the finished effect and determine the amount of shrinkage.

Choose a simple garment pattern with straight lines and a minimum number of seams. Patterns for bulky outerwear fabrics or patterns for loose-fitting, oversized styles are recommended, to allow for the bulk of the four layers. When cutting out the pattern, allow ⅝" (1.5 cm) seam allowances.

The seams may be sewn conventionally, right sides together. Or for decorative, exposed seam allowances, sew the seams wrong sides together. The outer edges of the garment may be left unfinished to complete the cut-and-curled look, or bound, as on pages 42 to 45.

Pullover has layered and slashed detailing. Rows of stitching were added across the slashes at 2" (5 cm) intervals for a more controlled effect. When inserting layered and slashed detailing, it is best to use two layers of fabric for the rest of the garment.

To prevent the fabric layers from shifting as you sew, reduce the pressure on the presser foot (page 29). An Even Feed™ foot may also be helpful to prevent shifting. Stitch, using a long stitch length of about 8 to 10 stitches per inch (2.5 cm).

Jacket, (opposite), made from four layers of interlock, has vertically slashed rows spaced 1" (2.5 cm) apart.

How to Sew a Layered and Slashed Garment

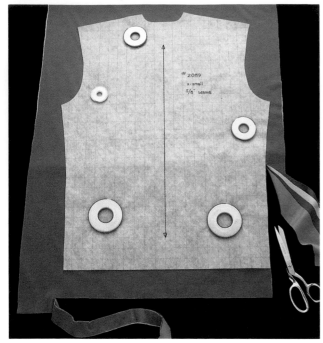

1) **Layer** fabrics in desired order on cutting surface, smoothing layers. Place pattern over fabrics; secure, using weights or pins. Cut, allowing ⅝" (1.5 cm) seam allowances; add extra length to garment sections to allow for shrinkage.

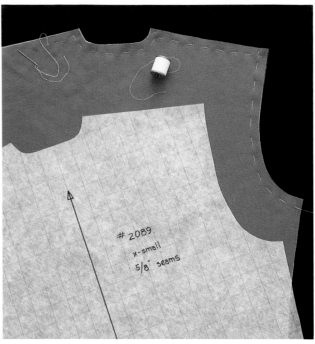

2) **Remove** pattern. Hand-baste fabric layers together ½" (1.3 cm) from raw edges.

3) **Mark** dotted center line on the garment back, following grainline, using chalk or water-soluble marking pen. Mark evenly spaced solid stitching lines. Lines spaced 1" (2.5 cm) apart work well for most designs.

4) **Match** garment front and back pieces at shoulder seams. Mark stitching lines on garment front to align with those on garment back.

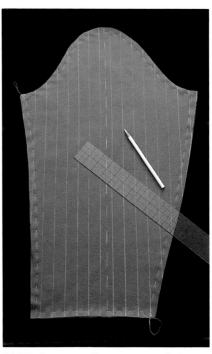

5) **Mark** center line on remaining pieces, along grainline; for sleeves, mark center line from dot at top of sleeve cap to lower edge. Mark stitching lines on both sides of center line, as in step 3.

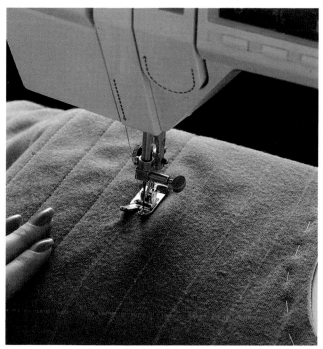

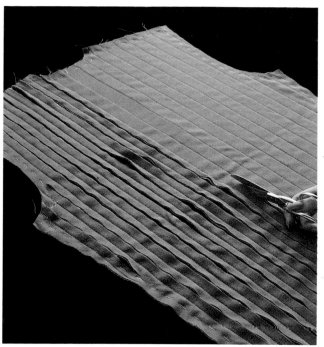

6) Stitch on marked stitching lines from top to bottom, working from center to sides of each piece.

7) Cut through all layers except backing fabric, midway between stitching lines, using sharp shears. Or, in some areas of the garment, in addition to the backing fabric, leave one or more layers uncut, to create an interesting design.

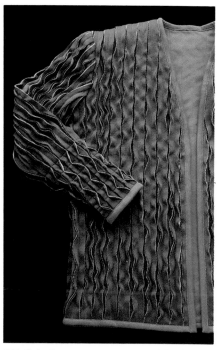

8) Mark and stitch across slashed rows, if desired, changing the direction of the slashed edges to create overall pattern.

9) Machine-baste seam allowances, securing slashed layers. Wash the garment sections and dry them thoroughly. Compare laundered garment sections to pattern pieces; shorten garment and recut armholes and neckline, if necessary.

10) Stitch garment seams. Bind outer edges, if desired, as on pages 42 to 45. Or trim seam allowances from outer edges and stitch two rows, ¼" and ½" (6 mm to 1.3 cm) from edges. Remove any exposed basting stitches.

Twisted Knit Trims

Twisted knit trim may be used to add texture and interest to garments along seamlines or edges, or to create free-form designs. The looped ends of the trim may also be used as a button closure.

Use single-knit fabrics that have moderate stretch, such as jersey, lightweight sweater knits, or French terry. The single-knit fabric can be cut either on the lengthwise or crosswise grain. When cut on the lengthwise grain and stretched, the edges of a single knit curl to the wrong side, resulting in a tube of fabric with the right side showing. When it is cut on the crosswise grain and stretched, it curls to the right side, resulting in a tube with the wrong side showing.

Cut fabric strips for trim from ½" to 3" (1.3 to 7.5 cm) wide, depending on how thick you want the completed trim to be. If the strips are cut on the crosswise grain, the combined length should be about two times the desired finished length of the completed trim. If they are cut on the lengthwise grain, the combined length should be about two-and-one-half times the finished length. Strips are pieced together as necessary, seaming them on the diagonal.

Before cutting strips for the garment, experiment with 24" (61 cm) lengths cut on the lengthwise and crosswise grains. Cut them at different widths, and twist to varying degrees to find the look you prefer.

Twisted knit trims vary in appearance, depending on the type of single-knit fabric used and the cut width of the fabric strips. Suitable fabrics for twisted trims are jersey **(a)**, French terry **(b)**, and sweater knits **(c)**. Metallic ribbon can be wrapped around twisted trim for a decorative effect.

How to Make Twisted Knit Trim

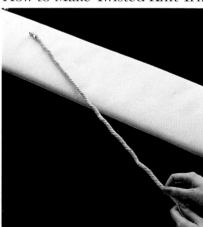

1) Pin one end of fabric strip to padded surface. Or have an assistant hold one end. Stretch strip as far as possible, so edges curl. Twist strip tightly.

2) Pinch strip at the center point. Bring two ends together, holding them to keep strip from untwisting.

3) Release hold at center; strip will twist itself into a single cord. Stretch and release cord to even out twists. Stitch across ends.

How to Attach Twisted Knit Trim to a Garment

1) Pin twisted trim in place on the completed garment; catchstitch in place, starting with loop end. Leave about 5" (12.5 cm) unstitched at opposite end.

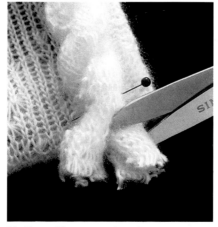

2) Cut off one cord as it passes under the other, as shown; hand-stitch to underside of trim.

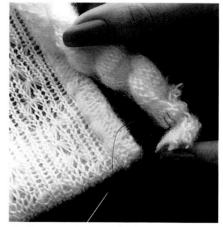

3) Curve other end of trim over and around first end; hand-stitch to underside. Finish stitching trim to garment.

Specialty Knits

Napped Knit Fabrics

Many napped knits look luxurious, but they are actually easy to sew. Included in the category of napped knits are velour, stretch terry, and stretch velvet.

When laying out the pattern, fold the fabric lengthwise, napped sides together. Place all the pattern pieces in the same direction. The direction in which the nap runs affects color shading in the garment (opposite). Keep in mind that the fabric may wear longer if the nap is smooth as it runs down.

Napped fabrics may shift during pattern layout and sewing. Cotton napped fabrics have less tendency to shift than synthetics, and those with a shorter nap are less likely to shift than those with a longer nap. The easy-to-follow tips (opposite) will help keep the fabric from shifting or marring as you stitch and prevent damaging the nap during pressing.

Napped fabrics include (left to right) crushed knit velvet, mediumweight velour with sheen, printed synthetic velour, stretch terry, lightweight velour with sheen, and cotton velour with matte finish.

Tips for Sewing Napped Knit Fabrics

Preshrink all washable napped fabrics, and machine dry them to fluff up the pile.

Use a long stitch length, about 10 stitches per inch (2.5 cm).

Pin napped fabrics at frequent intervals before sewing the seams, if necessary; this is especially helpful if the fabric tends to curl at the edges.

Remove pins from the fabric as soon as possible to avoid marring the fabric. Pin within the seam allowances whenever possible.

Stitch seams in the direction of the nap to keep the pile smoothed at the seamlines and to prevent the fabric from shifting.

Use an Even Feed™ foot or roller foot, if available, to prevent the fabric from shifting. Or reduce the pressure on the presser foot when using a regular presser foot (page 29).

Avoid the use of topstitching and buttonholes whenever possible, because of the tendency to mar the fabric or flatten the nap.

Sewing and Pressing Napped Fabrics

Decide which color shading you prefer before laying out pattern. If pattern is placed so nap feels smoother as you run your hand down toward lower edge, garment will be lighter in color and have slight sheen; in opposite direction, garment will appear darker in color and matte in appearance.

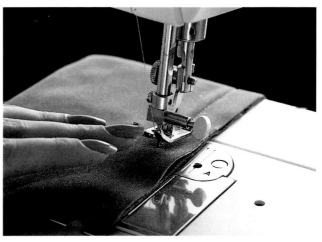

Stop stitching as soon as any shifting occurs. To correct shifting, raise presser foot and pat fabric to smooth it in place. Then lower presser foot, and continue sewing.

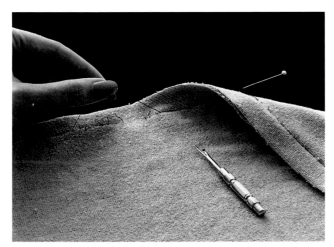

Remove stitches carefully to avoid damaging fabric. Cut stitches on one side of seam at ½" to 1" (1.3 to 2.5 cm) intervals, using a seam ripper. Pull thread from other side of seam; remove threads from first side, using soft brush or transparent tape.

Place self-fabric scrap or terry towel, right side up, on pressing surface, and place garment right side down. When pressing seams, prevent imprints on right side of fabric by placing paper strips or index cards under seam allowances. Or press the seam open on a seam roll.

Sweater Knits

Sweater knits are available in many fibers, weights, and knit types. They are divided into two categories: sweater bodies and sweater-knit yardage. Sweater bodies, panels with prefinished ribbed edges, are packaged with matching ribbing for the neckline. Sweater-knit yardage is purchased off the bolt; matching or contrasting ribbing yardage may also be available.

When sewing sweater knits, select patterns in simple styles with straight lines and gentle curves. Choose a pattern with a minimum number of seams, and eliminate seams wherever possible, such as at the center back of a straight-cut garment.

Cut the garment sections with ¼" (6 mm) seam allowances on the neck edge and with ½" (1.3 cm) seam allowances for the remaining seams.

When cutting and sewing sweater knits, avoid using pins whenever possible. They are easily buried in textured sweater knits, and if stitched over, they can damage sewing machine needles and serger knives.

When sewing sweater knits on a conventional machine, prevent the seams from stretching by using a long stitch length and by reducing the pressure on the presser foot (page 29); do not stretch the fabric as you sew. An Even Feed™ foot or roller foot is also helpful in preventing stretched seams. Double-stitched seams (page 29), using the zigzag stitch, are the most frequently used seams for sewing sweater knits on the conventional machine.

When sewing sweater knits on an overlock machine, use a medium-to-long stitch length and a wide stitch width. To prevent the seams from stretching, use the differential feed if your machine has this feature, or ease the fabric under the presser foot as you stitch by holding it loosely in front of the presser foot.

For seams that have built-in stretch, a 3-thread overlock stitch or a 4/3-thread mock safety stitch may be used. For stable overlock seams that do not stretch, the 4-thread or 5-thread safety stitches may be used; these stitches work best in securing loosely knitted fabrics.

Whether you are sewing on a conventional or overlock machine, it is recommended that you stabilize the shoulder seams (page 31), using transparent elastic or topstitching.

Sweater knit fabrics are available with coordinating trims. Sweater bodies **(a)** are prefinished panels of fabric that are sold in kit form with coordinating prefinished ribbed trims **(b)**. Sweater-knit yardage **(c)** is sold by the yard; coordinating prefinished ribbed trims **(d)** or ribbing yardage **(e)** may be available.

How to Cut a Sweater Body

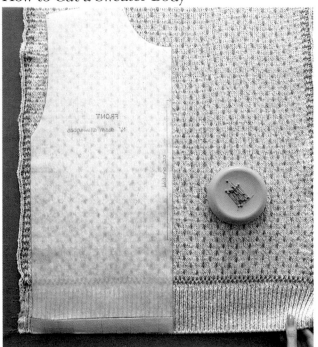

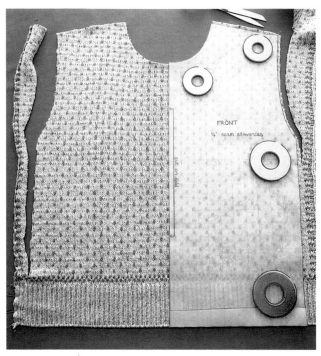

1) Lay sweater body on cutting surface that can be pinned into. Stretch ribbed edges to same size as body of panel; pin to cutting surface. Fold up hem allowance on pattern, if included. Lay pattern on fabric with fold at lower edge, along ribbed edge.

2) Cut, using single-layer method (page 25); allow ¼" (6 mm) seam allowance on neck edge and ½" (1.3 cm) seam allowances on remaining edges. Cut ribbing for neck edge using pattern guide, or by measuring neckline and cutting ribbing proportionately (page 35).

Tips for Sewing Sweater Knits

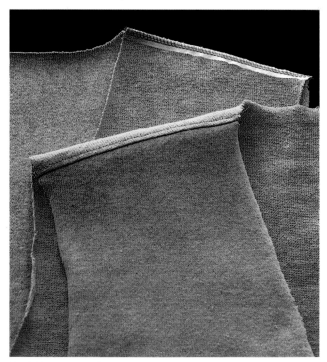

Stitch seams using overlock seam (page 30); for stable overlock seam, 4-thread or 5-thread safety stitches may be used. Or stitch double-stitched seams (page 29), using zigzag stitch.

Stabilize shoulder seams, using transparent elastic (top) or topstitching (bottom), as on page 31.

Sew sleeves to garment with sleeve cap facing down, easing sleeve into armhole; do not stretch the armhole to fit the sleeve.

Stitch ribbing to garment, with ribbing on top. Ease garment edge to match ribbing; do not stretch either the garment fabric or the ribbing.

Position buttonholes along lengthwise rib of sweater-knit fabrics to prevent stretching; stitch, stabilizing fabric with fusible web (page 65).

Steam press sweater knits, applying steam without touching the iron to the fabric. Avoid stretching fabric when pressing it.

Two-way Stretch Knits

Two-way stretch knits include an elastic synthetic fiber called spandex, which gives the fabric excellent stretch and recovery in both lengthwise and crosswise directions. The most readily available two-way stretch knits are nylon/spandex and cotton/spandex.

When sewing swimsuits, leotards, tights, and leggings from two-way stretch fabrics, be sure to select a pattern specifically designed for two-way stretch, because these patterns are sized so the finished garment will fit snugly without binding or sagging. Check the amount of stretch the fabric has against the stretch gauge on the pattern envelope (page 18). Stretch the knit crosswise and lengthwise to determine if the stretch is greater in one direction than the other. Nylon/spandex knits usually stretch more in the lengthwise direction; cotton/spandex, in the crosswise direction. Some patterns provide separate stretch gauges for lengthwise and crosswise stretch.

Two-way stretch fabrics are also used for skirts, tops, and dresses. For these garments, the two-way stretch fabric is used primarily because the spandex gives added body and drape to the garment, not because lengthwise stretch is needed in the garment. Patterns designed only for crosswise stretch may be used instead of those designed for two-way stretch; check the crosswise stretch of the fabric, as it will be worn, against the stretch gauge of the pattern. The same sewing techniques used for the easy wardrobe (pages 48 and 49) may be used when sewing these fashion garments from two-way stretch knits.

Select polyester, cotton-wrapped polyester, or woolly nylon thread for sewing two-way stretch knits. Some two-way stretch knits have a vinyl-like finish, as shown in the skirt, opposite. If topstitching is used on fabrics with vinyl-like finishes, stitch with the right side of the fabric facing down so the fabric feeds easily through the machine. If stitches are removed from vinyl-like fabrics, needle holes may be noticeable.

Although the shrinkage of two-way stretch knits is minimal, prewashing them is still helpful. If the fabric has become stretched or distorted while rolled on the bolt, prewashing restores it to its original knitted shape. Prewashing also removes any finishing chemicals, making the fabric easier to sew. Use the washing instructions provided by the fabric manufacturer, and allow the fabric to air dry. The heat of machine drying can damage spandex.

Two-way stretch knits are available in a wide range of fibers and textures.

Swimsuits & Leotards

Patterns for swimsuits and leotards are usually closely fitted for comfort and easy motion. A wide range of pattern styles is available. Styles with princess seams are slenderizing. So are patterns with a center panel of a contrasting color; to minimize hips, use a dark color for the side panels. High-cut leg openings on swimsuits and leotards give the appearance of longer legs and a slimmer torso. For a full-busted figure, choose a pattern with a bustline shaped by darts or seams. To fill out a slender figure, use a pattern with shirring, draping, or ruffles. Or choose a simple pattern style and a splashy printed fabric to enhance a slender figure.

By sewing your own swimsuits and leotards, you can make garments that meet your needs. Add a full-front lining (page 120) to a swimsuit, if desired; this is especially important for light-colored and lightweight fabrics. Or you may line just the crotch area (page 120) or add a bandeau lining in the bust area (page 122). Purchased bra cups may be sewn into the bandeau if firmer support is desired.

Two-way stretch fabric stretches to fit the contours of many different figure types. Select the pattern according to the bust measurement to avoid extensive fitting adjustments at the bustline. If you require different pattern sizes for the hips and the bust, choose a multisize pattern, following the cutting lines for the appropriate sizes and blending the lines in the waistline area.

Adjusting the Pattern

For one-piece swimsuits and leotards, measure your torso length as shown, below, and compare it to the torso lengths given in the chart at right; do not measure the pattern pieces for this comparison, because they will measure less than the actual body measurement. If your torso measurement falls within the range given for your bust size, no pattern adjustment is needed.

If your torso measurement is different from the length given in the chart, first adjust the pattern front an amount equal to one-fourth the difference, then adjust the pattern back the same amount. The total pattern adjustment is only one-half the difference between your torso measurement and the chart; the two-way stretch fabric will be stretched when it is worn, automatically giving you the rest of the length needed. If each pattern piece has two adjustment lines, divide the total amount of adjustment needed equally among all four lines.

Linings can limit the stretch of the swimsuit fabric, so if you are going to line the front of a swimsuit (page 120), add an extra ½" (1.3 cm) of length to the front and back pattern pieces.

Comparison of Bust Size and Torso Length

Bust size	Torso length
30" (76 cm)	52" to 54" (132 to 137 cm)
32" (81.5 cm)	53" to 55" (134.5 to 139.5 cm)
34" (86.5 cm)	54" to 56" (137 to 142 cm)
36" (91.5 cm)	55" to 57" (139.5 to 145 cm)
38" (96.5 cm)	56" to 58" (142 to 147 cm)
40" (102 cm)	57" to 59" (145 to 150 cm)
42" (107 cm)	58" to 60" (147 to 152.5 cm)
44" (112 cm)	59" to 61" (150 to 155 cm)

How to Adjust the Torso Length on the Pattern

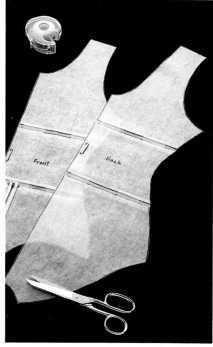

1) Measure from indentation at breast bone in front; bring tape measure between your legs to prominent bone at back of neck. Keep the tape measure snug to duplicate fit of finished garment. It is helpful to have someone help you take this measurement.

2) Determine the difference between your torso measurement and the torso length given in the chart, above, that corresponds to your bust size. The pattern needs to be adjusted an amount equal to one-half the difference; distribute this amount equally among the pattern adjustment lines.

3) Adjust the pattern, adding or subtracting length to the pattern by spreading or overlapping front and back pattern pieces on the adjustment lines, as on page 21. In the example shown here, front and back pieces are lengthened ¼" (6 mm) on each adjustment line for a total adjustment of 1" (2.5 cm).

Sewing Swimsuits & Leotards

Before laying out a swimsuit or leotard pattern, determine which direction of the fabric has the greater amount of stretch. Nylon/spandex knits usually stretch more in the lengthwise direction; cotton/spandex, in the crosswise. For a comfortable fit, lay out the pattern on the fabric so the greater amount of stretch will encircle the body.

Swimsuits and leotards are fast and easy to sew. Most styles have only a few seams and edge finishes. Stitch the side seams and crotch seam first; then try on the garment and adjust the fit as needed.

If a one-piece swimsuit or leotard is too long in the torso, shorten it at the shoulder seams; if this raises the neckline, the neck opening can be trimmed as necessary. If the armholes are too small, causing the garment to bind under the arms, enlarge them by trimming the openings. Leg openings should fit smoothly; if they are too large, take in the side seams at the lower edge, tapering the seams gradually. Stitch the shoulder seams after the fitting, and apply the elastic (pages 116 to 119).

How to Sew a Basic One-piece Swimsuit or Leotard

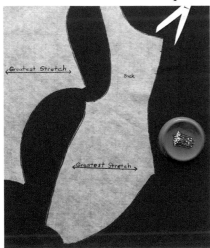

1) Determine whether the fabric stretches more on lengthwise or crosswise grain. Lay out pattern on fabric so the greater amount of stretch will encircle the body.

2) Stitch center back seam; then stitch crotch seam, applying crotch lining if desired (page 121). Stitch side seams. Check garment for fit, opposite.

3) Apply full-front lining, if desired (page 121). Stitch shoulder seams. Apply elastic to garment openings (pages 116 to 119); if making a swimsuit with bandeau lining, refer to pages 122 and 123.

How to Sew a Basic Two-piece Swimsuit

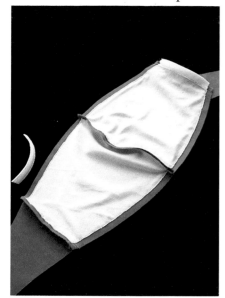  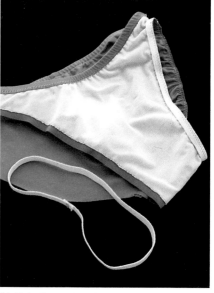

1) Lay out the pattern as in step 1, opposite. Stitch seams, and machine-baste lining to wrong side of swimsuit top, basting a distance equal to width of elastic from raw edges; trim lining close to the stitching. Center boning, if used, on side seam allowance, positioned so the ends will curve away from body. Stitch over previous stitches along inner edge of boning.

2) Apply elastic to edges of swimsuit top (pages 116 to 119). Make straps (page 118); stitch to garment, using narrow zigzag stitch. Pull right end through swimsuit hook, folding ½" (1.3 cm) to wrong side; zigzag across end. Fold left end ½" (1.3 cm) to wrong side; zigzag in place. Garment details, such as center front detail, are sewn following pattern.

3) Stitch center back seam of the swimsuit bottom. Apply full-front lining, if desired (page 121). Apply elastic to upper edge and leg openings of swimsuit bottom (pages 116 to 119).

Adjusting for a Good Fit

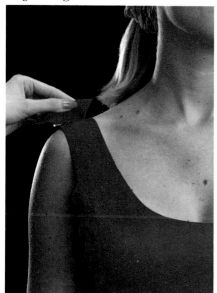  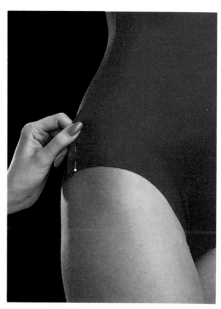

1) Adjust shoulder seams for snug fit if garment is too long in torso. Adjust neck opening if shoulder adjustment raised the neckline, marking adjustment with chalk, then trimming on marked lines.

2) Adjust armhole openings if the garment binds under the arms, marking the adjustment with chalk, then trimming away excess fabric.

3) Adjust side seams, if necessary, so leg openings fit snugly before the elastic is applied.

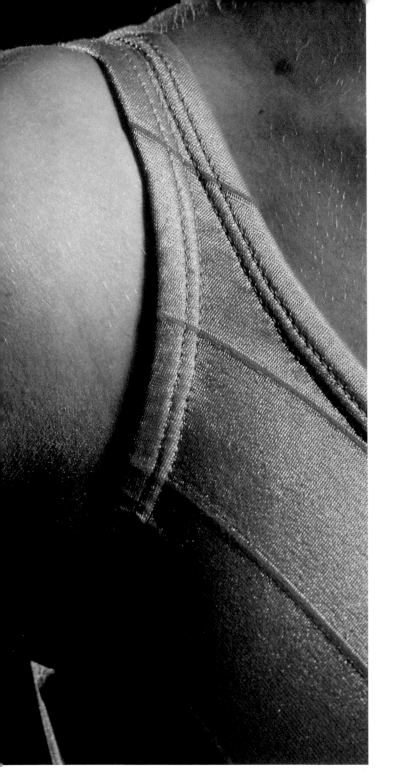

Elasticized Edges

To stabilize edges and to ensure a snug fit on swimsuits and leotards, use elastic at necklines, armholes, waistlines, and leg openings (opposite) or add an elasticized binding (page 118). Elasticized edges also allow you to slip the garment on and off easily. Although elasticized edges do self-adjust to your figure, do not depend on them to solve fitting problems.

If you have not adjusted the neckline, armhole, or leg openings, cut the elastic to the lengths specified by the pattern. If you have changed the size of the openings, follow the guidelines given in the chart below. Most patterns print the cutting information for the elastic on the guide sheet or provide a cutting guide on the pattern tissue. If using a pattern with several views, be sure to cut the elastic for the style you have chosen; for example, a high-cut leg opening requires longer elastic than a standard leg opening.

Cotton braided swimwear elastic or transparent elastic may be used. Both types of elastic, with excellent stretch and recovery, are chlorine-resistant and salt-resistant. Most patterns call for ⅜" (1 cm) elastic for adults' swimwear and ¼" (6 mm) elastic for children's.

Guidelines for Cutting Elastic

Type of Edge	Length to Cut Elastic
Leg opening	Measurement of leg opening minus 2" (5 cm) for adult's garment or minus 1" (2.5 cm) for child's.
Upper edge of two-piece swimsuit bottom	Measurement of upper edge minus 2" to 3" (5 to 7.5 cm), depending on desired fit. Check to see that elastic fits comfortably over hips.
Armhole	Measurement of armhole.
Neckline	Measurement of neckline. Or for a snug fit on V-necked, low, or scoop necklines, use elastic 1" to 3" (2.5 to 7.5 cm) shorter than neckline.

How to Apply Elastic

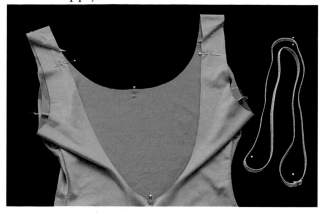

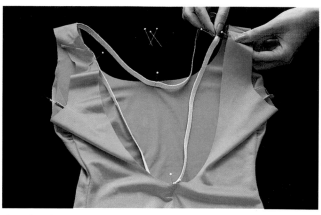

Neckline or waistline openings. 1) Join ends of elastic, using overlapped method (page 90). Divide elastic into fourths; pin-mark, with one pin next to joined ends of elastic. Divide garment opening into fourths; pin-mark. Seams may not be halfway between center front and center back.

2) Pin elastic to wrong side of fabric, matching edges and pin marks. Place joined ends at center back of neckline or waistline.

3) Stitch outer edge of elastic to the garment, using overlock or narrow zigzag stitch; stretch elastic to fit between pins. If using overlock machine, guide work carefully or disengage knives to avoid cutting elastic.

4) Fold elastic toward inside of garment, encasing it in garment fabric.

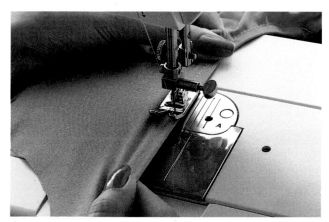

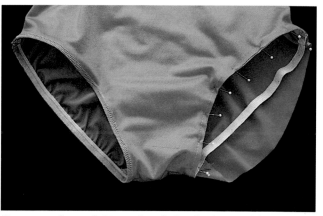

5) Stitch through all layers, ¼" (6 mm) from folded edge, using long straight stitches or narrow zigzag stitches, stretching as you sew. Or topstitch, using double needle.

Leg openings. Join ends of elastic (page 90). Pin elastic to leg opening, with joined ends at side seam, keeping elastic relaxed on garment front; remaining elastic will stretch to fit the back of leg opening. Follow steps 3 to 5, stretching elastic as you sew.

Elasticized Bindings & Straps

For a decorative finish, use elasticized bindings on a swimsuit or leotard, and make coordinating straps. Use the same fabric for the bindings and straps as was used for the body of the garment, or use another two-way stretch fabric in a contrasting color. The width of the elastic determines the finished width of the bindings and straps; cut the fabric strips in the direction of the greater stretch.

How to Make Elasticized Straps or Ties

1) **Cut** elastic the finished length of strap or tie plus 1" (2.5 cm) for securing ends. Cut fabric the length of elastic and four times the width. Without stretching the elastic, zigzag one edge to the wrong side of fabric strip.

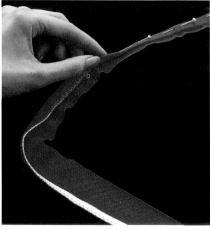

2) **Fold** elastic over twice, toward wrong side of strip. Pin the fabric snugly around elastic.

3) **Stitch** through center of strap, using double-needle topstitching. Or stitch using straight stitch, stretching as you sew. Trim excess fabric close to stitches.

How to Apply Elasticized Binding

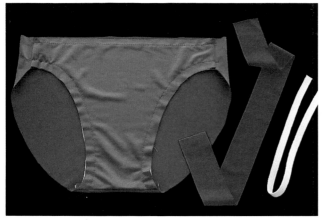

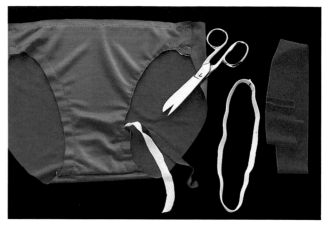

1) Cut elastic, depending on type of garment opening (page 116). Cut fabric strip for binding equal to the length of garment opening plus ½" (1.3 cm); cut the width of the strip equal to four times the width of the elastic.

2) Join ends of elastic (page 90). Join ends of fabric strip in ¼" (6 mm) seam. Trim garment edge to be bound an amount equal to width of elastic.

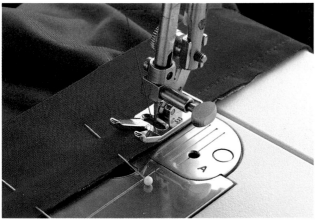

3) Place fabric strip on garment, right sides together. Baste ¼" (6 mm) from raw edges, using long, narrow zigzag stitches.

4) Pin elastic to garment as on page 117, steps 1 and 2, pinning it to the wrong side of fabric strip. Stitch along inner edge of elastic, using a long, narrow zigzag stitch.

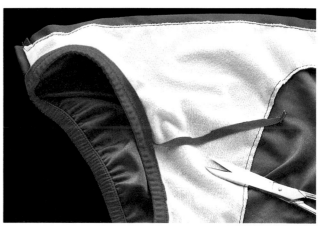

5) Trim seam allowances of fabric strip and garment to a scant ¼" (6 mm); be careful not to cut into elastic as you trim. If using transparent elastic, do not trim seam allowances.

6) Fold binding over elastic to wrong side of garment; pin as needed. Topstitch binding in place, stretching as you sew. Trim excess binding on wrong side.

Lined Swimsuits

Swimsuits, as a rule, are only partially lined, keeping the garment as lightweight, cool, and comfortable as possible. Some swimsuits have lining in the entire front of the suit for a smooth appearance and to prevent show-through when the swimsuit is wet. A full-front lining is especially important if the swimsuit is made from lightweight or light-colored fabric. For two-piece swimsuits, the full front of the swimsuit bottom can be lined, using this same technique.

Some swimsuits are lined only in the crotch area, and others have lining in the bra area, called a bandeau lining (page 122).

Swimwear linings, usually white or flesh tone, have two-way stretch. They are available in various types, from lightweight knits that are very stretchy in both directions to mediumweight knits that have limited stretch to provide control.

If heavier or limited-stretch lining is used to line the full front of a swimsuit, add ½" (1.3 cm) extra length to the swimsuit front and back pieces when cutting the fabric (page 113), to ensure a good fit.

For easier elastic application, the lining is basted to the swimsuit at the garment openings. If you are using the elastic method on pages 116 and 117, baste a distance equal to the width of the elastic from the raw edges. If you are using the binding method on pages 118 and 119, baste a distance equal to the width of the elastic plus ⅛" (3 mm).

How to Add a Crotch Lining to a Swimsuit

1) Cut crotch lining 5" (12.5 cm) long; use swimsuit front pattern as a guide for cutting crotch seam and sides.

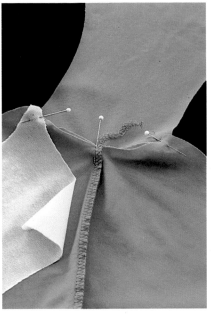

2) Pin crotch seam of swimsuit, right sides together. Place lining piece on swimsuit back, right side down, matching crotch seam; pin and stitch.

3) Fold lining toward swimsuit front, enclosing crotch seam. Baste lining to leg openings (opposite); trim lining close to stitches.

How to Line the Front of a Swimsuit

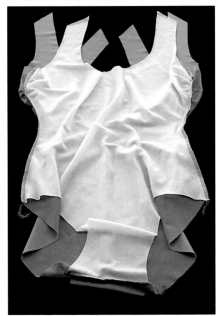

One-piece swimsuit. 1) Cut lining, using front pattern piece. Stitch side and crotch seams of swimsuit. Place right side of lining against wrong side of swimsuit back, matching raw edges; stitch side and crotch seams again. Trim seam allowances to ¼" (6 mm), if necessary.

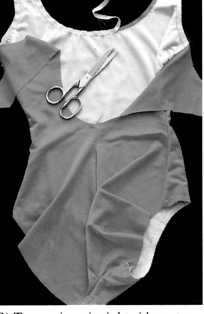

2) Turn swimsuit right side out; lining and front are wrong sides together and seam allowances are enclosed. Baste front and lining together at garment openings (opposite); trim lining close to stitches. Stitch shoulder seams, and apply elastic (page 117) or binding (page 119). Remove basting.

Bottom of two-piece swimsuit. Follow step 1, left. Turn right side out; lining and front are wrong sides together and seam allowances are enclosed. Baste front and lining together at upper edge and leg openings (opposite); trim lining close to stitches. Apply elastic (page 117) or binding (page 119). Remove basting.

Swimsuits with Bandeau Linings

Add a bandeau to line the bodice of a swimsuit for a flattering, smooth fit. Purchased bra cups can be stitched into the bandeau, if additional support is desired.

Use two-way stretch swimsuit lining (page 120) for the bandeau. Cut the bandeau with the greater amount of stretch across the width of the bandeau. For bust sizes 28" to 40" (71 to 102 cm), cut the bandeau 8½" long by 20" wide (21.8 by 51 cm); for sizes 41" to 46" (104 to 117 cm), cut the bandeau 11" long by 22" wide (28 by 56 cm).

For a comfortable fit, use ¾" (2 cm) felt-backed swimwear elastic at the lower edge of the bandeau. Cut the elastic 2" (5 cm) shorter than the width of the bandeau.

How to Add a Bandeau to a Swimsuit

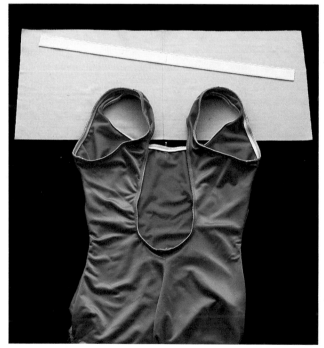

1) **Pin** and stitch elastic to neckline and armholes of swimsuit, as on page 117, steps 1 to 3, or as for elasticized binding on page 119, steps 1 to 4. Mark center of bandeau, felt-backed elastic, and swimsuit front.

2) **Pin** elastic to lower edge of bandeau, nonfelted side of elastic against right side of bandeau; match center markings and ends. Stitch, using zigzag stitch, stretching elastic to fit. Trim excess fabric close to stitching on wrong side.

3) Try on swimsuit; pin bandeau in place, with right side of bandeau against body. Matching centers of bandeau and swimsuit front, smooth bandeau toward neckline and armholes. Remove swimsuit, and adjust placement of pins as needed.

4) Stitch bandeau to swimsuit through center of elastic at neckline and armholes, using wide, long zigzag stitch. Stitch sides of bandeau to side seam allowances of swimsuit, using short, narrow zigzag stitches. Trim excess bandeau fabric. Finish applying elastic as on page 117, steps 4 and 5, or as for elasticized binding on page 119, steps 5 and 6.

How to Add a Bandeau with Bra Cups to a Swimsuit

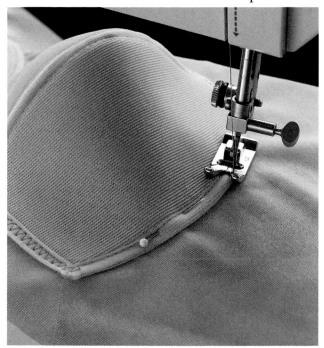

1) Follow step 1, opposite. Pin bra cups to wrong side of bandeau, spaced slightly apart on each side of center mark, with lower edges of cups 1" (2.5 cm) from lower edge of bandeau. Stitch cups to bandeau around entire edge of each cup, using zigzag stitch.

2) Turn bandeau over. Trim away bandeau fabric around bra cups, within zigzag stitching. Complete as in steps 2 to 4, opposite.

Tights & Leggings

Tights and leggings are popular for dance, active sports, and fashion garments because of their warmth, comfortable fit, and sleek lines. Tights, with or without stirrups, are generally made from lightweight two-way stretch fabrics. Leggings, made from heavier two-way stretch fabrics, do not have stirrups.

Use ¾" (2 cm) cotton braided swimwear elastic or knitted elastic at the waistline of tights or leggings. If you are using braided swimwear elastic, cut the elastic 2" to 3" (5 to 7.5 cm) shorter than the waistline; for a knitted elastic, cut the elastic 3" to 5" (7.5 to 12.5 cm) shorter than the waistline.

To ensure sufficient length in tights and leggings, add 1" to 2" (2.5 to 5 cm) to the waistline and 1" to 2" (2.5 to 5 cm) at the knees (page 21). Try on the garment after the basic seams are stitched, and make any necessary length adjustments.

How to Sew Tights and Leggings

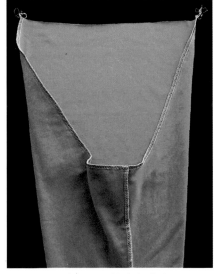

Without stirrups. 1) Stitch inseam of each leg, using overlock seam (page 30) or double-stitched seam, using zigzag stitch (page 29). Place one leg inside the other, right sides together. Stitch the crotch seam from front to back in one continuous curve.

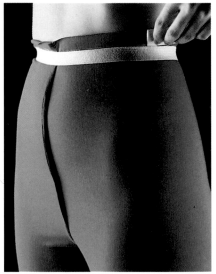

2) Join ends of waistline elastic, using overlapped method (page 90). Try on garment, wrong side out, with waistline elastic placed at natural waistline. Mark garment along upper edge of elastic. Remove elastic and garment; turn right side out.

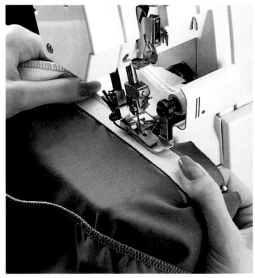

3) Divide elastic and upper edge of garment into fourths; pin-mark. Pin elastic to wrong side of garment, matching pin marks, with lower edge of the elastic on marked line. Stitch along upper edge of elastic, using overlock or zigzag stitch, stretching elastic to fit; if using zigzag stitch, trim excess fabric above waistline.

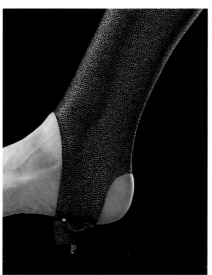

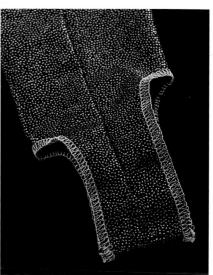

4) Fold the elastic to the wrong side, encasing it. Stitch through all layers, using 3-step zigzag or wide zigzag stitch and stretching elastic as you sew. Finish lower edges with ½" (1.3 cm) hem.

With stirrups. 1) Follow steps 1 to 4, except do not hem lower edges in step 4. Try on tights to determine the placement of instep seam. Pin both seams, using safety pins; test comfort by bending and stretching. After adjusting fit, stitch instep seams, right sides together.

2) Finish curved stirrup openings at bottom of tights, using overlock stitch or topstitched hem (page 33).

Index

Cy DeCosse Incorporated offers
sewing accessories to subscribers.
For information write:
  Sewing Accessories
  5900 Green Oak Drive
  Minnetonka, MN 55343